Praise for
Building the Good School

"Educators, parents, and communities who are ready for a new vision of education and change are fortunate to have this book for information, reference, and especially for inspiration." —Nancy Berla, National Committee for Citizens in Education.

"This is an inspiring story of a school community—parents, educators and students—working together to define and redefine their educational goals. As they strive to replace obsolete assumptions about curriculum, testing, literacy, and professionalism with a holistic understanding of teaching and learning, they discover the complexities and subtlties involved in this new approach. There is no easy recipe, no shortcut to building a genuine community of learning: It is a very human process that requires a spirit of cooperation, negotiation and mutual respect. But the Charquin story shows us that the result is well worth the effort. Indeed, as author Gloria Fearn demonstrates through numerous delightful examples, Charquin is a school where imagination, creativity, and personal experience are allowed to flourish; children, parents and teachers find empowerment and encouragement. Fearn concludes—correctly, I believe—that the Charquin School 'demonstrates a process which shows promise of transforming the way that we think about and act within schools.'" —Ron Miller, founder of Holistic Education Review, and author of *What Are Schools For?*

Building
the Good School
Participating Parents at Charquin

Gloria Wilber Fearn

RECEIVED

JUN – 3 1994

MSU - LIBRARY

Ohlone Press
Hayward, California

Building the Good School
Participating Parents at Charquin

By Gloria Wilber Fearn

Photos by the author
Cover design by Bob Newey
Back cover photo by Kate Jordahl

LB
1029
. 06
F43
1993

Published by
Ohlone Press
Post Office Box 779
Hayward, California 94543-0779

© 1993 by Gloria Wilber Fearn

All rights reserved. No part of this book may be reproduced or transmitted in any form or by any means, electronic or mechanical, including photocopying, recording or by any information storage and retrieval system without written permission from the author, except for the use of brief quotations in a review.

First Printing 1993
Printed in the United States of America

Library of Congress Catalog Card Number: 92-84077
ISBN 0-9635804-0-X

DEDICATION

To my mother who first showed me that a parent can influence the system.

and

To Bob, Norma and the parents of Charquin who nurtured and taught my child and showed me how to Build A Good School.

ACKNOWLEDGMENTS

To thank everyone who has helped with this book over the last five years would be nearly impossible. Writing this book has been a learning process through which my thinking has changed countless times. There were eight completely different versions of this manuscript. I am most grateful to Robert Whitlow who read and commented on most of the versions. Our long and frequent conversations shaped and reformed my thinking and writing in basic ways.

Norma Oden, David Ott, Julie Harcos and Jon Hassell gave the project time, attention and careful reading. Karen McCutcheon was open and helpful in discussing her role as a teacher in the program.

Kathleen Devaney and Lois Bridges Bird provided encouragement and asked important questions at various points along the way. Helena Worthen went above and beyond the call of duty in proofreading the project.

Early on, before I decided to focus this book on Charquin, I was considering doing a more general book about alternative schools. The parents, teachers and administrators from the Pine Crest Alternative School in Sebastopol and The Alternative Class in Pacifica assisted in my research. Mike McBride and Will Aubin of Pine Crest were particularly helpful in framing the issues.

During this early research my good friends Gail Bunker, Gregg Micheaels, and Gloria Wilson, who were serving on the Hayward Unified School District Board of Trustees, discussed with me their perceptions of Charquin and the role of alternative schools in public education.

The enthusiasm and support of Charquin parents, past and present, has made this book possible. Names and photographs of some of them and their children appear on the pages. Bob Newey, whose children graduated from Charquin, designed the cover. Many parents read and commented on the manuscript at various points in time. Without a doubt I will leave out several important names. Those who come most immediately to mind are Cheri Boulton, Linda Dandel Cano, Bernie Homen, Dick and Laura Hunter, Linda Jaster, Catherine Lamm, Alice Masek, Elaine Respass-Parsons, Karen Rogge, and Sherry Smith.

I also thank my husband and sons, Dean, Neal and Justin, and my father, Frank Wilber, who kept me motivated.

Contents

Introduction

For years it has been suggested that everything would be all right in the schools if only parents would do their job. But there's little agreement on what that job is. Some people would limit parents to enforcing strong discipline and backing up the teachers. For others the job gets much more complex. They say parents should read to kids, help with homework, attend parent-teacher conferences, PTA meetings, and band concerts, buy the candy bars that PTA sells in order to raise money for field trips and library books, feed their kids a nutritionally balanced diet—not including candy—get them to bed early, practice positive parenting, read and respond to notices from the school nurse, librarian, teacher, principal, counselor, and the director of elementary education, chaperone dances, guard the gate, and staff the snack bar at athletic events, monitor the hallways during lunch, supervise the bus stop, and guard the class floats against pranksters on Rally Day. Those who hold this more expansive view of the job of parents advocate parent participation in the classroom and sometimes even suggest that parents should be allowed to teach.

There is good evidence that those who argue for parent participation in the schools are on the right track. Anne Henderson of the National Committee for Citizens in Education compiled a list of nearly fifty studies which suggest that parent participation in schools improves student achievement and is a positive force for school reform. Unfortunately, the relationship between parent participation and school reform at times seems circular. Not only is parent participation a positive force for school reform, but schools must reform in order to encourage parent participation. The rules, environments, and critical attitudes toward parents which characterize many schools discourage parent participation. These are systemic problems—rooted in the assumptions of an out-dated philosophy on which the school system was built.

This out-dated philosophy comes to us from the nineteenth century and early twentieth century, when our rapidly industrializing nation was not worried about school drop-outs, and had lots of jobs for the minimally educated. The philosophy was rooted in a *technological world view* (Clark), and guided by a mechanistic theory about how children learn. The mechanistic theory of learning assumed that knowledge could be broken up into small pieces (basic skills), poured in by the teacher, and evaluated with paper and pencil tests. The instructional goal was a sort of *mechanical literacy* (Sherr) which was thought to enable a reader to decode words, sequence events, and recall facts. The process depended on individual student and teacher effort and a competitive ethic.

The crisis in our schools relates directly to the persistence of this outmoded world view, a view which assumes that a technological approach, focused on basic skills and delivered by professional educators, will prepare students to meet the future. The basic skills approach, in attempting to remove the child from the context of his family and community, has left children and their parents disempowered, needy, and too often illiterate. Furthermore, the isolation of teachers has made teaching a discouraging business.

The critique of schools has long focused on low test scores and high drop-out rates. More recently the focus has shifted to one which calls into question the traditional purposes and methods of schools. In part this shift has occurred because business has come to perceive its needs in new and more demanding ways. Today's workers must be powerfully literate and socially competent. They must be able to manage information, communicate ideas, and work well with others in defining, researching, and developing solutions to problems. (U.S. Dept. of Labor)

But business is not the only critical voice. This past political year brought to the attention of Americans the serious problems of many of our society's institutions. In his book, *The Good Society*, Robert Bellah discussed the problem of reconstructing our institutions, and spoke of the importance of developing schools that are "democratic learning communities," schools that engage us with the moral and technical problems of the day. Bellah says, "It is certainly not enough simply to implore our fellow citizens to 'get involved.' We must create the institutions that will enable such participation to occur, encourage it, and make it fulfilling as well as demanding."

Ron Miller, in his book, *What Are Schools For?* struck a hopeful note is saying, "There is mounting evidence that a new paradigm—an entirely new worldview—which is more ecological, global, spiritual and, in a word, 'holistic,' is rising to meet the challenges of the late twentieth century." Indeed, the philosophy that has made student learning and parent participation in schools difficult has started to crack. After twenty years of research into how children learn reading, writing, spelling, and mathematics we see the emergence of a more holistic, constructivist theory of learning.

The constructivist view is that children construct, within themselves, knowledge and rules about the language that they use. They do not adopt this knowledge directly from external sources. (Manning, Manning, and Kamii, p. 4) Constructivists see language learning in holistic, developmental terms. They hold that learning to read, write, and do math are a natural part of language development, and are accomplished through the same process by which children learn to talk. On their way to becoming literate, children pass through many stages and make many mistakes. Their mistakes are helpful clues to their thinking and progress as they re-invent and learn to apply the rules of their language.

The Whole Language Movement is bringing constructivist learning theory into the classroom. The role of the Whole Language teacher is to make accurate assessments of where the student is in his learning at any given moment, to provide a rich context for learning, and to ask questions that promote empowerment and trigger higher level thought. Experience and reflection are at the center of a Whole Language program. Children are credited with knowing a lot and with having a desire to learn. Because of its concern for empowerment, and for the context of learning, Whole Language has a deep commitment to democratic process and to parent and community participation in the schools.

This book tells the story of the Charquin *(CHAR-KEÉN)* Program. Charquin is a public school program in Hayward, California. The program is dedicated to parent participation. It was founded in 1973, and based on the then popular Open Classroom Model. The Open Classroom Movement and the Whole Language Movement were similar in that they both had their "...roots in the work of John Dewey and Jean Piaget,..." (Smiley). The Charquin story is timely both because Charquin demonstrates the issues involved in parent participation and because in recent years Charquin has adopted much from Whole Language.

In the Beginning

The Charquin Program is named after a rebel who is remembered in history books as Northern California's first Native American hero. Charquin's claim to fame is that he escaped from the mission in San Francisco in 1793, crossed San Francisco Bay, and organized a band of warriors. For the next twenty years Charquin and his men made life difficult for the padres at Mission San Jose. Like this rebel, today's Charquin Program has always bucked the system. Boxes, jails, and filling in the blanks are not for Charquinites.

The Charquin Program was originally located at Laurel Elementary, a public school in Hayward. It has since moved to Markham Elementary in the same district. Opening the program required almost two years of planning and work by parents from Humpty Dumpty Parent Co-op Nursery and the California State University Children's Center. In the beginning Charquin was a multi-age grouped, parent-participation, Open Classroom. The program had thirty kindergarten through third grade children, the parents of most of them, and one teacher, Celestine Randall Villa, working together in two adjoining classrooms.

After one year the Board of Trustees declared Charquin to be a success and allowed it to expand. Robert "Bob" Whitlow, a first year teacher, was hired to teach the second class. Charquin encountered all of the problems that were so typical of alternative public schools. Parents argued. The district was hostile. Enrollment declined. At the end of the second year the program was cut back to thirty students. Celestine moved on to another school in the district, and later became an elementary school principal. Bob stayed to get Charquin organized.

Bob was Charquin's only teacher until September of 1984 when the program expanded to serve sixty students through the fifth grade. At that time Norma Oden joined the faculty. The younger children were Norma's primary responsibility. In 1987 Charquin expanded once more, reaching its current enrollment of ninety students. Amy Hafter joined the teaching team and spent two years at Charquin. Amy decided that she would rather have a self-contained classroom. She moved to another room at Markham. Karen McCutcheon, a third year teacher who had been at Markham for one year, took Amy's place on the Charquin faculty.

Charquin Philosophy

From the beginning Charquin was notable not only for its holistic, Open Classroom structure, but for its remarkably high level of parent participation and its intensely democratic practice. Charquin students and parent participants are members of a dynamic family which has taken on new concerns and new directions over time.

In philosophy the Charquin Program now sits somewhere between the Whole Language model and the Open Classroom model. This has not been a trivial change. While Open Classrooms and Whole Language classrooms share a common holistic philosophical foundation, the two approaches are different in some important ways.

Bess Altwerger (19) clarifies the relationship between the two approaches with this observation:

> Both Open Education and Whole Language note the active character of learning; both center on 'the whole child.' Both see learning as rooted in firsthand experience and genuine problem solving. Both concern themselves with more than language and literacy, more than thought or learning in the abstract but with thought-in-interaction, with learning-in-life. Significant content provides a curricular focus in Whole Language as well as Open Education.

Altwerger (20-21) goes on to point out the differences between Open Classrooms and Whole Language classrooms. In Open Classrooms organization is more often structured around learning centers or committees. "Scheduling in Whole Language classrooms is more closely tied to the task (e.g., writing workshops, science project work)." Open Classrooms emphasize individuality, while "Whole Language views the learner as profoundly social." Both theories reject standardized tests, but for different reasons. Open Education sought to develop democratic classroom communities within non-democratic larger contexts. The goal of Whole Language "is (the) empowerment of learners and teachers,..." Whole Language holds "that increased democracy within individual classrooms must accompany work on understanding and changing larger contexts."

In its early years Charquin ran true to the form that Altwerger suggests. One of Charquin's early documents, *Philosophical Basis and Characteristics*, (1975), reflects a holistic philosophy.

> Learning begins at birth. Learning is continuous....personal... purposive ...self-motivated...requires that material be appropriate to the child's level of development...requires that the child be the director, not the receiver,...requires the active participation of the child.

Charquin emphasized individualized instruction rather than cooperative instructional strategies. Charquin's founding documents use the word "cooperation" only once, and then in a context which made it clear that protecting the individual from the negative effects of competition was the point. The program viewed itself as an alternative to the system, rather than as a force for changing the system. It was assumed that the classroom would practice democracy, but that as an alternative school, Charquin would influence other classrooms only to the extent that the district chose to use the program as a "laboratory of learning."

Early on Charquin parents developed learning centers in the classroom and set policy in the Parent Group. Some of the learning centers were: computers, cooking, gardening, music, art, language arts, drama, science, math, sewing, P.E. and puppetry. In 1983 or '84 parents decided to organize curriculum units around social studies themes. Charquin students took many field trips and had much contact with the outside world. Traditions grew.

In recent years Charquin has moved in the direction of becoming a Whole Language program. In so doing philosophical issues and practices have at times been matters of hot debate. A recent document, *Charquin Philosophy,* places more emphasis on community-building and cooperation than did the original statement. It begins with the words:

> Our basic goal is to provide an enriched, holistic program where children, parents, and staff can learn and work together to nurture and stimulate self-esteem, creativity, social, emotional, physical and academic growth and well-being.

> Charquin is a place filled with the sounds of activity and laughter. It is a continuously changing community which is actively engaged in educating itself. Charquin community members are accepted, encouraged, and made aware that they are important. Their experimentation and risk-taking are encouraged. Charquin is a link between the home and school, a family oriented place where long term friendships flourish.

Charquin's philosophy demands a certain attitude, and has implications for program management and classroom practice. It means that:

• Charquin should have no remedial readers, and no remedial math students. This is not to say that all children will read and do math equally well. It is to say that each child should be respected as an individual, and as an important member of the community—that she should be encouraged to use reading, writing, and math as tools to learn what she needs to know.

• Children should not be measured against a standard, or against each other.

• The classroom must provide children with many opportunities to find meaning in their world. They must be offered a wealth of information, encouraged to question, and to explore issues of importance to them.

• Children should be attended to and encouraged, but they should not be given awards and inducements for good behavior and obedience to rules.

• Children should be trusted to make choices, to decide which centers they want to attend, and what topics they want to research and write about. They should learn to manage their own learning, and use their literacy to effect change in their world.

• Charquin parents should have an active voice in and responsibility for the program.

In Search of Whole Language

From the beginning, Charquin's holistic, Open Classroom philosophy required that children be allowed to make many choices. It also assumed that they would become literate while in school.

Unfortunately, Charquin's founders also subscribed to the then popular—but incompatible—mechanistic view that becoming literate is a matter of learning basic skills. "Learn basic skills" was item number one under "Content" in the document that the school board approved when Charquin was authorized. This same document stipulated that the children would take state mandated tests, tests designed to support the basic skills approach.

Since the basic skills approach requires much teacher-directed instruction and supervision and allows students to make few choices regarding their activities, it set the stage for conflict among participants, some of whom were concerned about basic skills and others who were concerned that children should be free to make choices.

During Charquin's third year Bob needed control and parents were tired of fighting. Bob took a strong hand and established basic-skills methods. He grouped students more or less by ability and required them to move from center to center with their groups. He used the district's basal readers and workbooks in math and spelling.

The new regime was a mixed blessing. The scheduling often interrupted students who were working in centers. These interruptions called into question both the children's ownership of the learning process and the value of the parents' work in the centers. But district administrators welcomed the new structure. Charquin students developed a reputation for achieving high test scores. The program soon had a waiting list. But the debate continued. The Parent Group took up the issue at least a couple of times a year. Some parents pushed Bob to loosen up. Others liked the security of the system. Since everyone liked Bob, they gave him latitude.

After several years Bob became bored with the basic skills approach. He did loosen up. He started doing what Yetta Goodman calls "kidwatching." He developed his own, more experiential method for teaching reading. He let go of the basals. He allowed students to make individual choices about their participation in centers—with a few requirements attached. Bob returned to school. In the Advanced Reading and Literacy Leadership Program (ARLLP) at UC Berkeley, Bob encountered Whole Language philosophy. Bob watched his own daughter learn how to read by writing, and how to write with invented spellings. He "felt like Buddha peeking over the wall."

During the past seven or eight years Charquin teachers and parents have been testing process-oriented instructional approaches which support Whole Language philosophy. The Bay Area Writing Project, The Bay Area Math Project, Family Math/Equals, Math Their Way, and the McCrackens have all influenced the program.

As parents and teachers work with ideas and materials, they are constantly reflecting, communicating with one another and revising their ideas. As they work together the program changes. Today's program is more holistic and child-centered. The "skills" are generally subordinated to the purpose of learning significant content and practiced in context. Basal readers and math workbooks are infrequently removed from the shelf. When they are, the lesson is planned to meet a specific need, a need that has been demonstrated by a child's work. At Charquin learning and teaching is a cooperative, interactive process.

The Charquin Program is not a place for philosophical purists. It's much like a crazy quilt. The general philosophy, and especially the reading and math programs, have a Whole Language flavor. The learning centers hearken back to the Open Classroom. Not all that happens in the centers is holistic. Some parents still have a skills-based teaching style. As Ken Goodman (1986, 69-78) points out, becoming a Whole Language program is in itself a process. Usually teachers work at it one bit at a time. Parents go through the same process.

Charquin is still growing. Charquin's teachers and parents are working hard to do as Judith Newman (1) suggests that they should: they are seeking to "explore the practical ramifications" of this philosophical stance that we call Whole Language. They are doing it in their own way.

Change Isn't Easy

Over the years I have repeatedly heard Charquinites say, "At Charquin change is the only constant." At times it seems as if this might be true. Indeed, when alumni return they are often dismayed at the magnitude of the changes. Both the philosophy and the methods and practices through which the group seeks to live out that philosophy have evolved and are continuing to do so.

Charquin's democratic, participatory structure challenges teachers to grow and to exercise professional leadership. As teachers learn and grow professionally they want to try new things. If they're going to do this they must convince parents and prepare them to help. That means having persistence, patience and good answers to the questions that come up.

At times change is a very difficult and emotional process. I have often heard it said that "Charquin runs on trust." Democracies—particularly those that exist within the context of a larger, undemocratic system—depend on participants who share an understanding of their goals, purposes, and history. When leadership or conditions change too radically, members dig in; they become fundamentalists who grasp at symbols and won't move.

When Bob promoted the use of cooperative learning strategies in math, he found out how difficult change can be. For some parents, having children spend more time in cooperative math groups and less time in their centers brought into question the value of the parents' participation. They didn't like that. Suggesting that these parents could take the Family Math workshops and help out in math, where some of them weren't comfortable, was threatening. Cooperative learning in math eventually became an established practice, but not without a lot of parent education and some considerable pain.

On other occasions change has been attempted, met with resistance, and everyone has fallen back to re-group. On one such occasion Norma Oden proposed doing away with her reading groups, so that she could spend more time orchestrating literacy events across the curriculum, and working with parents to encourage writing in the centers. The idea was that this plan would more clearly link reading to the purpose of learning significant content, and would make it more natural and meaningful—in short, holistic.

Unfortunately, the plan precipitated a crisis of faith among parents, who didn't trust themselves to teach reading and weren't sure that children would learn to read unless Norma's supervision was regular and frequent. In the end Norma made some changes, but not as many as she had hoped.

There are certain critical times in the life of an alternative school. The loss of a key faculty member is one such time. Program expansions, when a large number of new members and teachers join the program, is another. The Charquin Program has expanded twice since 1984, tripling the number of students in the program from 30 to 90, and likewise tripling the number of participating parents and teachers.

These expansions were made doubly difficult because not only did they bring in new members, they also brought in older students, changing Charquin from a K-3 program to a K-6 program. As a consequence of these expansions, scheduling became a more complex matter. This changed the feel of the program from that of a small intimate family to one of a larger, less intimate tribe. This matter of how the program felt was a difficult one for parents and for Bob, who valued the "old Charquin," and for whom the larger tribe presented a more complex leadership task. Another troubling issue was the question of whether the learning centers were developmentally appropriate for older children.

In the "old Charquin" (the program that existed prior to the first successful program expansion in 1984) everyone met around the same rug several times a day to read stories, discuss happenings, follow-up on instruction, sing songs, and take care of administrative tasks. Parents staffed learning centers for much of the rest of the day. Centers were designed so that children of all ages could participate, each at his own level and in his own time frame. Bob spent much of his time working with reading groups.

At first there were few special provisions made for younger children. (Although parents eventually started the "Rainbow Center" for kinder-gartners.) Kindergarten children participated in field trips alongside the older children, and in all other activities that were scheduled during the morning hours. For the most part they did fine, often sitting for long periods to listen to stories that traditional kindergarten teachers would have considered too advanced. Older children helped them along when the going got tough. A kindergarten child sitting on a third grader's lap was not an unusual sight.

In the wake of two program expansions there was a long period of resisting change and trying to hang onto tradition. In the summer of 1990 the teachers took the bull by the horns and scheduled some reorganization meetings. Parents and teachers spent several days working together in an effort to address the issues that the expanded program presented. They agreed that older children needed a different type of program but also needed to stay within the Charquin family.

This agreement lead to a new plan. Older children and younger children would meet in different rooms and have quite different programs. Older children would spend much of their time in a program which emphasizes cooperative learning, regular participation in Writers' Workshop, and the completion of big projects in various fields of inquiry. The program for the younger children would still be scheduled around centers. There would be more parents in Norma's room, both because of the larger number of centers, and because the parents of younger children tended to be more involved in classroom activities.

Different programs for older and younger children not withstanding, an effort would be made to allow all age-groups to mingle with some freedom within Charquin. Many activities (music, drama, cooking, field trips, snack, etc.) would include all students. And, older children would still help younger children with their journals.

When the plan was tried in the Fall of 1990 it proved difficult in some respects. For older children, scheduling took a more Whole Language format. The length of periods depended on the task at hand. In the younger children's program scheduling took a more Open Classroom format. A set block of time was designated as Centers Time and each child moved from center to center individually until time ran out. The consequence of different scheduling priorities for the two groups was that in most cases program-wide activities were worked in around Centers Time. The scheduling of these activities required constant negotiating among teachers. As often happens at Charquin, the plan was tried and revised—again, and again.

While the classroom schedules and organization were becoming more complex the Parent Group was likewise becoming more organized. Subcommittees and grievance procedures were established and a handbook was written.

And the challenges continue. In the fall of 1991 Bob left Charquin for a teacher training position in the Equals/Family Math Program at the Lawrence Hall of Science at the University of California, Berkeley. David Ott came to teach the older children. At the same time Jon Hassell, Principal of Markham School, transferred to another school within the district. Sharon Ough became the principal of Markham. At the end of the 91/92 school year Norma Oden retired. At the same time, David left, a victim of district-wide teacher lay-offs that sent teachers with more seniority than he had scrambling for positions. The district dispensed with parent participation in teacher selection and gave little consideration to matching the philosophy of the teachers that they assigned to that of the program. These actions by the district have threatened Charquin's viability as an alternative school, and brought parents together to redefine the program and explore their options.

Participants

Charquin is not the product of an affluent neighborhood. Nor is it located on a university campus. Charquin developed in a public school system with a class size of thirty students per teacher. Charquin is not a rich kids' school. Hayward is a blue-collar city on the east side of San Francisco Bay. Hayward Unified is a "new majority" school district, where no ethnic group comprises more than fifty percent of the population. In 1990 district enrollment was forty-four percent white, twenty-seven percent Hispanic, fourteen percent black, eight percent Asian, and five percent Filipino. Fifty-two languages are spoken by HUSD students.

This is not to say that Charquin students are not in some ways a special population. As with other alternative schools, there is an element of self-selection. Students can only attend if their parents can arrange transportation. During the last five or six years Charquin has had a long waiting list, so there is also a program selection process. Charquin practices affirmative action. Students whose siblings are currently enrolled and students whose parents say they will participate in the classroom also get special consideration. While the racial and ethnic backgrounds of Charquin's students are similar to those of the larger district and Charquin students are not particularly affluent, they are less likely to be poor or bilingual and more likely to live with two parents than are other district students.

While Charquin's general population is not exceptional with regard to the educational attainment of their parents, four or five years ago two noted educators were, for a time, participants in the Charquin Program. The leadership of Dr. Ruth Parker and Mary Laycock has left a deep imprint on Charquin. Mary took a leading role in educating parents about the uses of manipulative materials in math, and Ruth helped parents understand and apply cooperative learning strategies.

Recognition

In 1988 Charquin's reading and language arts program won a Golden Bell Award for excellence and innovation from the California School Boards Association. In 1990, Robert Whitlow won the Good Neighbor Award from the National Council of Teachers of English. The garden has won several grants and two National Gardening Awards. Science and puppetry programs have likewise received grants to support their innovative approaches. Students from the University of California at Berkeley as well as other universities are frequent visitors in the Charquin classroom. UC Berkeley has placed student teachers at Charquin. Dr. Richard McCallum and Dr. Charles Ulster used Charquin's literacy program as the subject of their doctoral dissertations at UC Berkeley. In his dissertation Dr. McCallum documented a high level of reading proficiency among older Charquin students. He also reviewed reading test scores and found that Charquin students tend to achieve higher scores with increasing age.

Importance of Charquin's Story

Six years ago when I first decided to write this book, I encountered resistance from an unexpected source. Some Charquin parents questioned whether a book about Charquin would be useful to a wider audience. They pointed out that Charquin is incompatible with the larger school system. Charquin grew within the system when nobody was looking. Building Charquin has been a long and arduous process. Other parents in other places would be hard pressed to copy Charquin. Some parents even pointed out that Charquin isn't perfect. At times it isn't even what it claims to be. As the saying goes, "Charquin is Charquin."

Of course the parents are right. It would be unrealistic to assume that all schools can develop Charquin's high level and quality of parent participation. But all good schools require hard work over a long period of time, and the Charquin experience has something to say to those who would advocate parent participation in the schools.

The Charquin story illustrates the importance of parent participation and structural issues that have been debated in the school reform movement ever since the publication of Goodlad's *A Place Called School,* in 1984. Charquin shows how parent committees, schools within schools, site-based planning, multi-age grouping, learning centers, and team teaching work to empower parents, teachers, and children.

Describing Charquin one piece at a time is a little like describing an elephant one part at a time. The model and the structural issues that it presents are important. But there's more there than meets the eye. Charquin is a living thing, a community which is held together and defined not only by its philosophy, methods, and structure, but also by its rich tradition, spirit and attitude. At its heart is the process of teaching and learning together.

It is difficult to write about Charquin's current practice, both because there is so much going on in the program, and because Charquin changes so quickly. Eighteen to twenty parents work in the program on a typical day. Every day they bring in new ideas and issues. The first chapter of this book is a story based on an observation that I did in the spring of 1990. Photographs and descriptions of activities were collected over several years, beginning around 1984. They are meant to be illustrative of philosophy and practice. The learning centers described here are ones that operated for at least several years; most are still in operation. They are only a sample of the program.

In telling this story, I make no special claims of objectivity. My perspective is colored both by my background in teaching and by my history as a Charquin member. Bob Whitlow complained that the book emphasized his story, while giving inadequate attention to the other teachers, which it does. I worked and talked with Bob regularly over the six years that my son was in his class. Bob Whitlow, Norma Oden, David Ott, Julie Harcos, Jon Hassell, and nine parents read and commented extensively on the manuscript as it passed through many revisions. Their comments helped form and refine the book.

At a time when educators are inundated with meaningless data, and schools are in search of goals, methods, and systems of evaluation with which students, teachers, and parents can identify, I hope the Charquin story, together with my analysis of it, will fit together and serve as a resource for parents and educators, helping them to work productively together in developing good schools.

"Good Morning"

At 8:15 A.M. Tuesday morning it's not clear that Markham School houses the Charquin Program. The school on the court at the end of Ward Street looks much like any other public school in California. It's a single story structure, with windows across the front where the janitor's room, library, principal's office, and nurse's office are located. On the left side of the building flags wave from the pole between the multi-purpose room and the main building. On the right is a kindergarten play yard, screened from view by a fence and trees. The classrooms are in the rear and the buildings are connected by breezeways. There are about a dozen parking spaces on the court in front of the school. On the other side of the multi-purpose room there are another dozen or so spaces. The grass and the shrubbery, nurtured by the janitor, are slightly trampled.

This morning the building seems inviting. Sunshine.... birds... polished floors. The retired bell from the original Markham School sits below a window which looks out on a little-used patio and a small lawn surrounded by bushes.

Gargi Shah, a slight-built, energetic and outgoing young woman, has just said good-bye to her five-year-old daughter, Tejal. The little one is down in room 10 where Roxanne, a Charquin parent, is doing "Morning Watch." On a usual morning there are fifteen or twenty children from the Charquin Program who arrive between 8:15 and 8:45 A.M. Since the yard is unsupervised until 8:45, a Charquin parent provides child care for the program's children during this half hour.

Morning Watch didn't used to be necessary when school started at 8:30 A.M. This year the opening time was changed to 9 A.M. and something had to be done. Many parents have to go to work or take older children to the intermediate school early. Since the Charquin Program attracts children from all over the district, it's not possible for children to wear latch keys or go to the neighbors' house for a half hour and then get themselves to school. Parents at Charquin are used to working around the inconveniences that the system imposes. They don't like Morning Watch, but they do it for the children.

On some days one of the seven parents who take turns supervising Morning Watch provides an art activity for children to do while they wait. Room 10 is the art room, and the environment presents children with lots of possibilities. Today the children are just entertaining themselves. They climb up and down on the two-story playhouse structure. Early arriving parents, like Gargi, wander in and out. Several of those who came for the day stop to visit. Others send their kids to morning watch and go to other rooms where they set-up their learning centers for the morning.

Gargi's comfortable leaving Tejal with the parents at school. She's known them all for a long time. It's an open environment where lots of people see what's going on. Unlike so many working mothers, Gargi doesn't have to worry about whether Tejal got to school in a safe and timely manner.

As Gargi rushes out the front door of Markham School on her way to her job at a bank in San Leandro, she reflects on what a good year this has been. After eleven years of taking care of babies, she's ready to leave her children and work part-time.

Gargi's older daughter, Laju, has spent the year going to school with relatives in India. Gargi's anxious for Laju to return home. Laju will have good stories to share with her friends at Charquin next year.

A big blue van pulls up and double parks behind the Vanagan which occupies the handicapped stall on the court just outside the entrance. This breaking of the rules is not officially sanctioned, but the powers that be don't look. Markham is now a crowded school with three portable buildings. In addition to the usual staff and visitor parking, spaces are needed for the eighteen or more parents who participate at Charquin on a usual day.

Judy Opilowsky's just staying a minute and doesn't want to take up space that a teacher, or one of the day's participating parents might need. She and her sons, Taylor and Morgan, climb out of the van and join Ben Masek and Brian Slater as they yank the front door open and hurry through the entry. The children chat about one thing and another as they proceed past the principal's office and down the hallway in the Charquin wing to the right of the entry. The children join Roxanne, the parent in charge of today's Morning Watch.

Judy, a young mother with medium-long dark hair that bounces with the rhythm of her step, listens to the children's chatter and responds with a quick smile. She just stopped by to take a look at the ice sculpture that she helped the kids build on the patio yesterday. Judy will pick up a couple of things for her next lesson and touch bases with Bob Whitlow before she leaves to do her morning chores.

Bernie Homen, a third year Markham teacher, walks through the entry on her way from the office to her classroom in the next wing. Bernie's the treasurer for the Charquin Program Parent Group. Her second and youngest child will graduate from Charquin in June and will enroll at Bret Harte Intermediate School as a seventh grader. Lisa's graduation will end Bernie's eleven year career as a Charquin parent. Bernie greets Judy and the children as they enter, then goes on her way.

Bernie often reminds her friends that it was her experience participating at Charquin which encouraged her to return to college, finish her BA, and earn a teaching credential. Now Bernie teaches a 2nd/3rd combination class. As one of the new teachers she's been switched around several times and has taught three different grade levels in three years. Bernie still loves teaching.

While Bernie runs a self-contained class, she is always on the look-out for new ideas and instructional strategies. She's an ardent believer in cooperative learning and manipulative math. Bernie helped develop Charquin's math program before she got her teaching credential. Her class often participates in Charquin's activities.

Elaine Respass-Parsons, a parent in her early forties with her hair braided in a traditional West African style, is talking with Jon Hassell in the principal's office. Elaine, a Charquin parent, is the Parent Group facilitator. She is a professional management consultant to businesses and non-profit corporations. The door is standing open, but their conversation is not overheard. They're probably fine-tuning some arrangements for the Parent Group.

Jon is a cheerful extrovert who shares inside jokes with teachers, staff, and parents. He has been Markham's principal for six years. The open door is Jon's symbol. Unlike other principals who minimize the importance of philosophy, Jon is committed to a holistic educational philosophy. When asked about his philosophy he uses words like "holistic," "child-relevant," and "experiential." He promotes parent participation, and got the Markham PTA started.

Being placed in charge of an alternative program that was characterized by some district administrators as a "squirrel cage" was a challenge for Jon. He works hard to move Markham's program in a more holistic direction. There's been plenty of foot-dragging, but progress has been made. Jon thinks the system can be changed from within, by chipping away. Jon's serious about the pursuit of change, and takes comfort in small things. He points out that this year Markham School faculty agreed that the school's goal "is to produce graduating sixth grade students who are able to solve problems, both academic and social, by working cooperatively." Faculty also spent several days evaluating their progress.

When Charquin wins awards and gains favorable publicity Jon makes the most of it and blows Charquin's horn quite openly. He enjoyed hearing a school board member use his words, "I want to Charquinize the world" in open meeting.

Elaine is one of seventy parents who volunteer in the Charquin Program. As Parent Group facilitator, Elaine walks a tightrope. Her main task is to help parents reach consensus on the issues that concern them. It's not easy getting eighty or ninety parents to agree on what they want on any given issue. When she meets success on that front she has to negotiate with administrators on behalf of the group. The process takes a lot of time and patience.

After Elaine finishes with Jon, she proceeds down the hallway to the easel which stands across the hallway from Bob's room. The easel holds a boldly written invitation to the evening's math workshop, together with sign-up sheets. Elaine can't attend. She's glad that her husband can, and signs him up. There's also a sign-up sheet for children who will need babysitting. Babysitting for the meeting will be provided in the art room.

Bob calls from inside his room to Linda Dandel Cano, who's stopped to sign up for the workshop. "Hey, if I don't get over to Laurel, please see that my kid gets signed up for the pottery class."

"I'm sick today. I don't know whether I'll go over there or not."

Linda's the mother of Travis. Her older daughter, Dana graduated last year. She's just dropped Dana off at the intermediate school, and is now leaving Travis at Charquin. Linda plans to do a couple of quick things and then go home. If it were not for this pesky germ, she'd be on her way to

Laurel—the district's adult school—where she teaches parenting and crafts classes.

Linda proceeds down the hall to Norma's room where she gives Norma a bright yellow Viola Swamp sweatshirt. Linda decorates sweatshirts as a hobby. Viola Swamp is Norma's Halloween character— a scrawny, witchlike school teacher.

Norma beams, "Oh, thank-you. I really wanted that shirt when I saw you wearing it the other day." She pulls off her cardigan, pulls on the sweatshirt, and gives Linda a big hug.

Linda protests, "I'm sick." They both laugh, and Linda proceeds down the hall to room 10 where Morning Watch is nearly over. She sits at a table with a couple of pieces of construction paper, some glue, and scissors, and tries out an idea that she wants to use with the kids next time she comes. She's not satisfied with the results, but puts away the materials and leaves for home.

By now Bob and Norma are in the office signing in, picking up their mail, and joking with the office staff and other teachers about one thing and another. Norma asks Bob whether a certain day would be a good time to schedule a speaker on psychomotor development. The speaker is someone she wants the parents to hear. Norma wants to make certain that the date doesn't interfere with the older students' science camp preparations. Bob can't remember exactly what's on the calendar for that day and agrees to get back to Norma. He steers his wheelchair out of the office and heads for his room. Elaine waylays him with a couple of quick questions about this evening's activities. Bob gives an abbreviated response as he cuts a tight corner. They proceed on their separate ways.

In 1974 when, as Bob puts it, he was "tall," Hayward Schools hired him as Charquin's second teacher. The founding teacher, Celestine Randall Villa, moved on to other things the following year. For the next nine years, until Norma came, Bob was Charquin's only teacher. Ten years ago Bob broke his back when he fell from a tree. He's been driving a wheelchair ever since. As Charquin's most senior teacher, Bob is mentor to everybody. Bob's job requires countless personal contacts with students, teachers, parents, administrators, and program visitors.

The hallway down which Bob travels makes a statement about the richness and diversity of the program that has required so much of his time and energy for so many years. The entire hallway is a gallery. Materials are taped, and even stapled to the walls, as well as to the bulletin boards.

While the hallway display is ever-changing and doesn't always hang together neatly, it serves several purposes. The hallway is a Parent Center where information about the program is shared and people gather to talk. The hallway display articulates the program's philosophy, illustrates current units of study, and shows off student work. In so doing it nurtures the self-esteem of Charquin members and encourages their sense of ownership.

Starting at the corner on the right, a row of poster-size tagboard calendars—one for each month—list program events. Above the calendars hang pictures of parents—black line drawings of their faces, traced on clear plastic. On the opposite corner, across the hall from the calendars, there's a friendship quilt made from construction paper. Below the quilt hangs a poster picturing a big red apple. It announces "All I Really Need to Know I Learned In Kindergarten." Next to the poster there's a quote from Fred Rogers (cited in Postman and Weingartner) which somebody ran off on a dot matrix printer. It reads:

> It's easy to convince people that children need to learn the alphabet and numbers....How do we help people to realize that what really matters...is how a person's inner life finally puts together the alphabet and numbers of his outer life.
> What really matters is whether he uses the alphabet for the declaration of war or the description of a sunrise, his numbers for the final count at Buchenwald or for the specifics of a brand new bridge.

Under the window, next to Mr. Rogers' quote, blue sheets of construction paper hang on the wall. Block letters which spell the name of a child run down the left hand side of each piece of blue paper. The child whose name the letters spell has used each letter as the first letter of a descriptive word. "Lovely, Entertaining, Special, Loveable, Incredible, Exciting," are Leslie's words.

Next to the blue sheets of paper hangs a big blue sheet of butcher paper with a title done in felt pen which reads, "The Charquin Family." The poster displays family pictures of many Charquin Program participants. The display looks a little worn, as does the origami limb of a flowering tree which hangs from the ceiling.

A long strip of butcher paper footprints, each one bearing the name of a child, are tacked to the ceiling beginning near the origami limb. The strip of footprints is nearly as long as the hallway. One end of the strip is hanging down.

Getting closer to Bob's room, blinds hang over the windows in the hallway to cut down on the glare for those days when the computers are set up in the hall. Across from the windows, letters cut from magazine pictures of greenery are pinned to one of the long, skinny bulletin boards. They announce "EARTH DAY EVERY DAY." A variety of Earth Day posters hang below the bulletin board.

A wire is attached to the wall outside Bob's door about five feet up from the floor. It runs down the hall to the corner, twenty or twenty-five feet. Student reports hang at children's eye level, suspended from brightly colored pieces of yarn tied to the wire.

The Parent Center is across the hall from Bob's door. The easel is there for important announcements and sign-ups. A chart rack sits next to the easel. As parents arrive they write what they plan to do today on the chart. The chart for this morning is already partially filled in.

Parent mailboxes of the office variety are stacked on a table. On top of the mailboxes are a dusty bundle of free magazines, a clipboard for items people want placed in the parent newsletter, and a shoe box covered with yellow construction paper. The shoe box is for concerns to be considered by the parent-teacher-liaison. On the floor next to the mailboxes sits a big garbage can and the box for collecting aluminum cans.

A parent bulletin board holds news clippings and announcements. The clippings include the story of a Charquin father who retired early to spend time at Charquin with his first grade son, a letter to the editor about hillside development written by a former Charquin parent, and a story about a Markham student throwing a pie in Jon's face, a reward for winning a school contest.

Announcements address a wide variety of participant interests and program needs. There's an invitation to an open house for the boys' choir in which a couple of Charquin kids sing, a class list, a notice of a missing library book that a teacher might have to pay for if it isn't returned, and various schedules and sign-ups. There is also a thank-you for earthquake assistance which was rendered by Charquin students to students in Watsonville.

Silliness and political messages adorn the hallway. On the window sill is a picture album of the "Dog Wedding." Last summer a group of Charquin families wanted an excuse to get together. Someone came up with the idea that Bob's dog could marry Cherie's dog. Everybody could get dressed up, pick flowers, and go to the park for the outdoor ceremony. The event was a hit, and somebody recorded it on film. The Far Side cartoon on Bob's door features a persistent individual pushing a door which is clearly labeled "PULL." The caption reads, "Midvale School for the Gifted." Harper's Index of the 1980s is there too. Bob captioned it: "A Catalyst for Rantings." Several weeks ago Bob spent some time ranting to some parents about what the survey showed about our nation's priorities. Then he posted it on the door.

As Bob navigates down this hallway toward a room where he has much to do, children and parents are gathering. He greets a couple of them before opening the door, and going to his desk.

If the Charquin Hallway is unusual, so are the program's classrooms. Most notably, they lack desks for students. Bob's room has a wood and vinyl sofa, some cushions, and several "centers." Each center has one or two large tables surrounded by chairs. A science bulletin board and related equipment on the countertop designates the table at the back of the room as the Science Center.

The walls of the classroom are covered with student work, charts, maps, and visual aids of one kind and another. The little center near Bob's desk is where he teaches his reading groups. One of the moveable cabinets has been positioned to separate this area off from the rest of the room. All of the centers are multi-use areas. They are used for different purposes by different parents and children at different times of the day. The children spend a lot of time sitting on the rug which dominates the center of the room.

As soon as Bob enters his room one parent after another comes in. Each one demands his immediate attention. At one point four parents are talking among themselves in the far corner of the room. Bob hurriedly puts finishing touches on something he was planning to use during one of today's reading groups. Since the parents aren't talking to him at this moment, maybe he can finish something before somebody else comes in. These types of interruptions would drive most teachers up the wall. Bob takes them in good humor—usually. He has learned over the years to be very clear about what he needs to do. He's not at all backward about asking parents to run and fetch things, correct a stack of papers, or help a kid in some way. His effective use of parents allows him to focus his energy on teaching, thinking, and managing.

Bob views himself primarily as a teacher of children, but he shares the instructional function with so many parents that training and supporting parents is basic to his job. Coordination with the other teachers and with school staff is likewise essential. Although he's never been given a title, much of the task of coordination seems to fall to Bob. His position in the first classroom means that everyone who walks down the hallway passes his door. They're often tempted to stop in. The task of coordinating is not a safe and sane one. At Charquin all members of the staff, and all parents have a real sense of ownership. It's the empowerment of the individuals that keeps the program going. There's a political content to coordination decisions, and a certain amount of lobbying takes place. Decisions about who gets to do what with whom and for how long requires an astute understanding of the values and feelings of the people involved. It also requires the ability to articulate educational priorities and philosophy clearly in ways that encourage cooperation.

Norma finishes up in the office and heads for her room, chatting along the way. She is a slim, blonde, young-looking sixty year old who plans to retire next year—maybe. Norma stops in at Bob's room to reassure herself that the schedule for the morning hasn't changed. She reminds Bob of a couple of fine points relating to the day's schedule. Norma joined the Charquin team six years ago when she moved from Tennyson Parent Nursery. The younger children are her major responsibility. Room 9 is her home base.

Norma walks out of Bob's room and proceeds down the hall past the big butcher paper sign with the hastily written message:

> ATTENTION Charquin friends
> Please do not use the copy machine
> Harry "Zerox"unless you check with the
> management.
> OK—OK
> Thank you

Another bulletin board, near Room 10, holds an announcement for Sam's Super Sitter Service. It also has newsletter banners and a picture of a car which was produced on the computer by a Charquin member. There's a letter from a Charquin family who is spending the year in Indonesia, a picture book of an excursion to the Outdoor Learning Center, and an announcement of a TV program on alternative schools. There's a big yellow piece of butcher paper on the wall which displays student writing. There are pictures and descriptions that children have written about themselves.

The cupboards sit in the hallway. They were moved out of the classrooms in order to provide more space for instructional centers. They now provide storage space for art supplies. A couple of tables and chairs sit next to the cabinets. They are used when children and parents want to work on special projects outside the classroom. Across the hall, next to the broom closet, hangs a poster showing the primary and secondary colors, with each color named in Spanish. There's a display of pictures that were taken when Charquin went on a field trip to the Steinhart Aquarium in Golden Gate Park.

Between the broom closet and the end of the hallway hangs a collection of manila folders. Each folder displays a picture or two of a child, his name, and several descriptive phrases in the child's own words. One folder has a picture of Norma's husband, Walt, with their grandchildren. It reads:

> 'Wally' Papa Walter
> Super Grandpa
> nice warm lap
> great story teller
> 63 years old
> blue eyes

Norma enters room 9 and goes to her desk near the window to work on a couple of last minute details. One of those big portable circular fences sits on the rug. It was set up yesterday when a fussy toddler didn't want to let his mother do her work. The children helped entertain the baby and have since enjoyed using the space themselves. First grader Andrew and second grader Austin are playing with plastic dinosaurs inside the fence. A parent is preparing a writing exercise in the language arts corner. Norma goes to the sunny reading corner behind her desk to pull out some materials for her first group. She chats with the boys in passing.

Norma loves visiting with people. She's much like a mother hen. When scheduling and curriculum decisions are made she makes certain that the little ones are not forgotten. Babies and toddlers are welcome in Norma's classroom, as long as things don't get out of hand. Sometimes students are allowed to spend a few minutes babysitting.

Norma has always spent a lot of time attending to the environment. Furniture and equipment is planned and arranged with little people in mind. Norma likes things neat, clean, visually pleasing, and well planned.

Between Bob's room and Norma's room is Karen McCutcheon's room. Karen's an energetic third-year teacher, in her first year at Charquin. 8:45 A.M. finds Karen standing in front of the yellow filing cabinet pulling out materials for an assignment. She's already been hard at work for forty-five minutes.

Morning Watch just ended. David's mother is helping him finish some homework. They're using the window sill as a table. Car pools are arriving outside. Unlike the rest of the children at Markham, Charquin children are entering through the front door. Children and parents are visiting in the hallway and filtering into the classrooms.

Two boys enter the room carrying a large rat cage between them. The rat runs around for a minute, then one boy takes him out, holds and strokes him for a minute.

Karen knows that she will have no more preparation time unless children go out to play. This year she started the practice of enforcing outside recreation before school.

"Everybody out," Karen calls over her shoulder. Karen holds her finger in the place in the file from which she has just removed an idea book. She looks at a page in the book for a second, decides it will do, and closes the drawer.

Jason, a sixth grader, and Brian, a fifth grader, linger to show Karen the "popper" they made from Popsicle sticks. They drop their toy so she can see how it pops apart on the floor. Karen watches with good humor. They giggle, and kneel down to gather the sticks.

Karen turns to go to her desk. All of the children leave, except David, who has permission to stay in. He sits down and holds the rat.

Karen taught fifth grade at Markham last year. She says that she's not really as open in her management style and instructional strategies as Bob is—at least not yet. She likes to work from specific plans, relies on textbooks a little more, and isn't always willing to go off on tangents at somebody's casual suggestion. Still, Karen considers herself to be more open than most teachers. Karen does worry about consistency and follow-up. Bob is more casual. He jokes that "In pigeons a variable rate of reinforcement produces more persistent activity." (Bob enjoys poking fun at behaviorist philosophy.)

Karen and Bob work closely together. They share most of the same third through sixth grade students. Karen values the time that Charquin teachers spend meeting and working together. She says that units which used to take only a few days to complete when she was working in a self-contained classroom now last much longer, are richer and deeper. The other teachers and parents give Karen many ideas for new things to try.

Unlike the other classrooms in the wing, Karen's and Bob's are not connected by an open doorway. While Karen can walk from her room into Norma's room and from there into the art room without going either outside or into the hallway, she must go around to reach Bob's room. When Charquin expanded from sixty to ninety students three years ago, it was decided not to have a doorway cut through into the new room. While younger children, their teachers and parents go to Bob's room often, and he shares the instruction of the older children with Karen, his room is the one where the door is frequently closed. In Bob's room older children pursue those writing, math, and social studies activities which require longer blocks of uninterrupted time.

Karen Rogge, one of the day's participating parents, comes in to let Karen M. know that she couldn't find the rat food on Friday afternoon when her son took the rat home. The teacher stops her preparations and looks to see whether it is behind the sofa where it belongs. It isn't. No matter, Karen R. had purchased some more.

Karen R. leaves. Karen, the teacher, returns to her desk, hopeful of being able to prepare a homework assignment before school starts. Today parents won't have to help kids with their homework. The assignment is simple and requires little writing. The directions read: "Make a banner showing how kids can conserve paper. Write a caption for the banner." The last couple of minutes before class slip by quickly. The bell calls children in from the playground and class begins.

The first thing Tuesday mornings all of the children and teachers gather in the art room for music. Norma is already in the art room near the piano. Alice Masek, the music parent, is seated at the piano. She's ready to start the singing. Karen is on her way to music, chatting with children along the way. Bob leaves his desk and gets to the door.

Barbara Archuleta, the parent who teaches Spanish, intercepts him. She needs to know when there will be a time for the group she's been working with to present a play to the class. Barbara's group has learned "The Three Bears" in Spanish. The play has to happen during one of the times when Barbara can be present. They set a tentative time, and proceed out into the hall.

A sixth grader who didn't turn in any work yesterday and didn't make much progress last week either passes by. Bob catches him and asks where the work is. Receiving no adequate response, Bob tells him to spend this time in room 7 getting the work done. The child is not to go to centers today until he is finished. Bob's irritated. Despite Bob's best efforts to encourage responsible work habits, this boy seems to demand constant supervision. His parents keep promising to help, but are inconsistent.

Leslie Sawyer-Long is discussing with several parents just how the fourteen or fifteen projects that parents have listed on the Centers Chart are going to interface. Leslie is today's "Rover." She's in charge of the chart. Leslie directs a question to Bob, who stops to study the problem. They agree—in typical Charquin fashion—to "Try it and see."

By the time Bob gets to Room 10, ninety children, Karen, Norma, Alice, and a half dozen or so other parents are gathered. Some parents are still preparing activities in their centers. The participants are tightly packed into the room. Most are sitting on the floor. Some students, scattered around the periphery of the room, are leaning against tables, or sitting on chairs. They are singing a rousing rendition of "Pollution." The group has already done a couple of other songs, and have little time left. The upbeat piano is accompanied by knee slapping and finger clicking. The song ends with coughing.

The children request "Teddy Bears' Picnic." The song's an old favorite. Alice digs through the charts on the music rack and flips to the chart with the words to the song. Bob is near the doorway, singing. After the song Bob takes notice of two older boys, one for his non-participation in the singing and the other for not having turned in his writing assignments for the past week. Bob makes his displeasure clear, then plays at strangling the non-writer. The group sings "Teddy Bears' Picnic" with enthusiasm, ending with giggling.

As music time draws to a close, Around the Rug begins. On music day the students stay together for Around the Rug, which is abbreviated and business-like. On most other days each teacher has thirty or so students in their own room.

Norma calls roll for her group, "Mr. Kidwell, Miss...."

Karen calls roll quickly. When she gets to the name of the student in Bob's room, Bob tells her where he is.

"What'd he do?" asks a little voice.

"It's what he didn't do," says Bob.

Giggling ripples through the group.

The roll continues as each teacher checks to see whether their charges are present.

Leslie arrives in the classroom during the song and sets the Centers Chart by the door, near Bob. When the singing ends Leslie reads the chart to the class and gives a brief explanation of unusual activities. Leslie asks the parents to tell about their centers.

Half a dozen parents say a few words about their planned activities, underlining special rules for the day, or saying why this activity is important. Kent Faulk, the cooking dad, is wearing a special green apron and chef's hat. He gives his spiel about the historical origins and importance of corned beef. St. Patrick's Day is coming up, and corned beef is being prepared in the Cooking Center today.

Bob underlines today's rule about the P.E. Center. "There will be no more than fourteen people on the field at the same time. You may only stay at P.E. for twenty minutes. This is a softball skills lesson. Hot shots needn't go."

The children are released from Around the Rug. For several minutes the milling around looks like the approach to the San Francisco/Oakland Bay Bridge at rush hour, when everyone is trying to get to the toll booth. Children who are scheduled to read or write with a teacher during the first period go in the direction of that teacher's center. Most children head directly for whichever activity they've decided to do first. A few children check with friends to see what they're doing before making up their own minds. Parents go to their centers. Leslie helps wandering children either get involved in a center, or find an alternative activity. This is Centers Time.

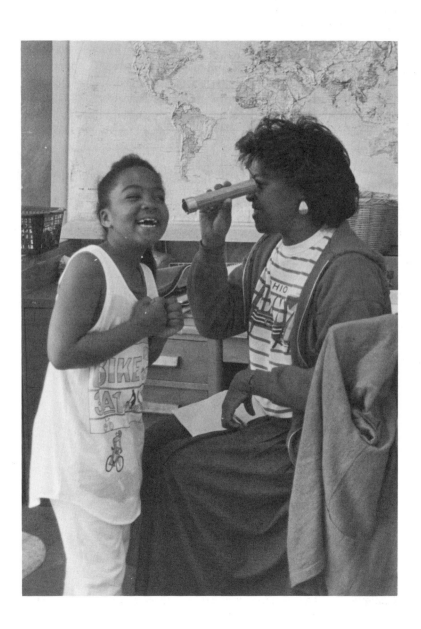

Parents Sharing Their Lives

One day I asked Bob, "What do parents do best?" His response came back with conviction, "They share their lives with children." Sharing really is the operative word when considering what Charquin parents do. And it's not a contrived, putting-in-the-hours type of sharing either. It's a sharing that challenges and stretches the parents as well as enriching the children.

At Charquin parents know that the program runs on participation. They have made the choice to participate. Often they postpone careers and live near the edge financially in order to spend more time with their children. And, it's not just mothers who make the sacrifices. Some fathers do too. The program supports parents in these decisions by providing them with the opportunity to participate in meaningful ways. It is understood that some parents can't participate in the classroom regularly and others may be available only on rare occasions. These parents work with teachers and other parents to develop a flexible schedule or to do tasks that can be done outside the classroom.

As parents share their lives, they are in fact teaching. The whole issue of parents teaching in a public school has political overtones. Over the years some school board members, teachers, and even some parents in Hayward have not always agreed that parents should be allowed to teach in the classroom. Teaching was seen as a professional task. In the early years Charquin stepped around the issue by calling what parents did "supporting instruction." But Charquin parents have always considered themselves to be teachers. Forbidding parents from presenting subject matter to children, or "teaching," seems counter productive and silly to Charquinites. The concern has quieted in recent years. Success counts.

Charquin's general format for parent participation is this: one parent, or other adult family member from each child's family signs up to work in the classroom one day each week. Families with more than one child often participate one day for each child (one half day for a kindergartener.) Participants may sign up to work in a subject-matter center which interests them, or they may develop a new center. They co-operate with each other, and with the teachers and students to develop curriculum in math, science, computers, language arts, physical education, art, cooking, gardening, dramatics, Spanish, ... and the list goes on. Some centers are intended only for a certain age group, while others, like cooking, art, and gardening, invite everybody. Many of these activities require much outside preparation and are testimony to the serious commitment that parent volunteers bring to the enterprise. Diversity and richness in curriculum are a big part of the Charquin experience and much of that richness comes from parents.

A goodly number of Charquin families lead lives which do not allow them to participate in the program according to the established format. In some cases both parents work all day. In others, a single parent is struggling to support a family alone. These parents look for things to do. They may prepare materials or check papers at home. They may do extra clean-up work after school, gardening, or a fund-raising activity. In some cases a parent may come in every day during a vacation or during a break in their work schedule. Sometimes they'll do a special project. Other times they'll just hang out and help where needed. Charquinites call this "alternative service." Some parents who can't participate donate to a special classroom fund. Donations are not solicited. Whatever parents can and want to do is appreciated.

With the participation of so many adults in the classroom, the line between teachers and parents and even between adults and children is less obvious than in more traditional classes. Each parent is assigned to be a special friend to one or two children. Teachers are called by their first names by everyone. They are most often found sitting in centers at children's eye level. Teachers are seen sitting on the floor working with manipulatives, or puzzles, or just talking with children. "Where's the teacher?" is the cry of visitors and participants alike.

Centers Time

Centers Time is a central feature of the Charquin Program for younger children. Mondays through Thursdays Centers Time happens immediately after Around the Rug, and lasts most of the morning. Friday is a cooperative learning day, when the age groups arc mixed and the teachers do their own thing, most often science or social studies projects. A couple of parents help out. The responsibilities of the children during Centers Time is age dependent. Older children spend little time in the centers, working instead on projects, research, and Writers' Workshop with Bob and Karen. They also do book math with Karen a couple of times a week. Kindergarten, first, and second grade children have few responsibilities. Younger students must participate in two or three centers and meet with their teacher for fifteen or twenty minutes if their reading group is scheduled. Some of the second graders, those who write well independently, may have a writing group. Students move among the different rooms at will, doing whichever activities catch their fancy. If they are just hanging out, the Rover will help them find something to do.

There is such a diversity of activities happening in the various centers that children seldom get to all of the centers. Children pick and choose, often not returning to a particular center on a subsequent day. Some children are a little like preschool nibblers, tasting a little of this and a little of that. Others may spend a lot of time in one favorite center and need coaxing to branch out. Some centers are described here; others are discussed in the chapter on Basics.

Cooking

Kent Faulk is Charquin's long-time cooking dad. Kent's center is noted for its ethnic flavor. There's not an ethnic holiday that goes uncelebrated in the Cooking Center—Chinese New Year, Hanukkah and St. Patrick's Day all get their due. Kent weaves geography and history into his projects. He often comes to Around the Rug in costume. My favorite is his Halloween costume, where he wears a real jack o' lantern over his head.

Aside from history, geography, and sociology, the Cooking Center provides specific math and science content. Children measure, add, subtract, and discuss ingredients which might be substituted in the recipe. They observe and discuss how flour, water, baking powder, yeast, and various spices work in combination, and what happens when these ingredients are heated, stirred, and cooled. Cooking is a science experience. Tortillas, tamales, won tons, latkas, pasta, rosettes, Navajo fry

bread, johnny cakes and ice cream are but a few of the delicacies that Charquin kids cook.

Since Charquin's last expansion there are too many children for one Cooking Center, so other parents pitched in to keep two Cooking Centers running simultaneously. They coordinate with Kent and do the same projects on the same days.

Gardening

The Gardening Center was started by Kent's wife, Leslie. The Charquin wing of Markham School has four adjoining classrooms, each thirty feet long. The back doors of the classrooms open onto a blacktop patio about twenty feet wide. Between the back edge of the patio and the next wing of the school is a piece of dirt. It used to be impenetrable hard pan and full of weeds. Leslie saw the possibilities. She scrounged for materials and money. She enlisted the help of Kent and other parents to build flower boxes and fill them with top soil. Leslie took classes through the Cooperative Extension Service. She wrote grant applications and obtained funding for her project. A composter, tools, and irrigation system were obtained. A compost bin was built. The garden gave a whole new dimension to the Charquin curriculum.

In Leslie's center children learn about the different parts of the plants and what the various plants need in order to thrive. They compost kitchen waste and prunings and talk about ecology. Students study worms and insects. They learn about landscape planning by drawing designs to determine the placement of plants. They vote on which plan is the best and use it when planting. Children record events on calendars and chart their results.

The Garden Center is an interdisciplinary, problem-solving experience. Children must learn something about chemistry in order to test the pH of the soil in different parts of their garden and determine what types of soil conditioners are needed.

Finding seeds and plants that will grow and ripen before school is out in the spring is a major problem, even in California. So, when a garden shop downtown went out of business, Kent purchased a display rack for seedlings. He hung a grow light on the rack. He placed the contraption in the art room, where seedlings are started for early transplanting.

Last year the Science Center parents coordinated their study of bugs with Leslie. In previous years the "Bug Lady," one of those marvelous community people who has a collection of bugs and a giant earth worm, came to school and spent a day with the children. The nutrition component in Leslie's Garden Center curriculum coordinates with Kent's cooking projects. The tomatoes are used to make sauce for pasta. The various vegetables and fruits are incorporated into other dishes as well. Children regularly participate in watering, fertilizing, planting, and weeding. Little feet are constantly among the rows looking for ripe fruits and veggies. While doing so they encounter snails, slugs, centipedes, spiders, earwigs, worms, and a rich variety of life which they might otherwise never notice. Teachers and parents gather next to the garden at lunch time to enjoy the sun and share ideas. The garden is a year 'round project which brings teams of children and parents back to school during the summer months for watering and harvesting.

Art

Charquin's Art Center is a very open place, staffed by parents who are serious about art. Art Center parents are some of Charquin's more freewheeling, outspoken and political members. Doing art requires space, organization and resources. If one participant doesn't put things away, or uses materials that were meant for someone else, everyone who uses the room suffers. Art Center parents get political when they feel crowded and resources aren't available.

Art Center parents have built their own environment. The art room is a beautiful place with recent projects displayed on the bulletin boards and colorful mobiles hung from wires. The Cooking Center is at one end of the room. The two-story playhouse structure is at the other end. Shelves have been built in the window cases where plants and projects are placed. Often several parents work in the Art Center room at the same time on different activities. They share ideas, visit a lot, and enjoy Kent's cooking.

Randy Vanderford loves drawing. He is a graduate of San Francisco Art Institute and is well acquainted with developmental stages in children's art. He once did a year-long drawing and painting project with students. Children learned about foreshortening steps and shading for perspective. They worked with acrylics regularly. At year's end many of the students had their work hung in Hayward's Festival of the Arts show downtown.

Randy is often seen lying on the floor with kids as they draw colorful monsters and fanciful designs of the type seen on skate shirts and skateboards. Anything can be a subject for drawing in Randy's center. When two little girls sit across the table from each other drawing portraits of one another they learn both technique and the observational skills that are central to art.

Several times Suzanne Cancilla did a year-long pottery project. Children came to her center to construct pots and animals from clay. She would take them to be fired and bring them back for glazing. The window sill was lined with clay constructions for most of the year. Children learned how to slip pieces together so that they wouldn't fall apart in the kiln. They learned how different glazes dried with different colors than were expected. They talked about the metals in the glazes that produced the colors.

Roxanne Padgett likes doing big constructions. Once she got Joe Silva to build a plywood and chicken wire frame for a giant dragon. The children spent a couple of weeks applying the papier-mache. Then they painted it. The beautiful creature stood in the entry way of Markham School for a year. A couple of years ago Roxanne spent three weeks doing giant marble paintings on butcher paper. Children cut the paintings into strips about three inches wide and experimented with weaving the strips together with other materials. Newspaper, yarn, strips of fabric, and even twigs were mixed with the painted strips. The wall hangings were so beautiful that some parents hung them in their livingrooms.

Cherie Boulton spent weeks last year helping every child make a piece of jewelry. Parents are still wearing the lovely pins that were produced. She's also the parent who came up with a way to make "dog barf" for Halloween. The recipe involved mixing kitchen bouquet, gelatin, and wood glue together, pouring the mixture out onto a piece of waxed paper, and dropping pieces of split peas and dog food into the mixture. The dried product, when dropped on the floor, looked exactly like dog barf.

Linda Dandel Cano likes making quilts. Quilts have been an on-going Charquin project. Every year the children design and make a big quilt which is raffled off at "See-Ya-Bye," Charquin's year-end celebration. This project has involved an on-going study of form, style, color, and history. Each year a different style is tried.

Computers

Several years ago, when a couple of computers first made their appearance at Markham School, Catherine Lamm was one of the few people who wanted to have anything to do with them. She would roll in three computers on her participation day and try all kinds of new things. Bob suggested materials and his friends at Lawrence Hall of Science sometimes made recommendations. Catherine did a lot of research too. She uses several Sunburst programs that are thought provoking. Catherine looks for programs that require problem-solving, and the use of reference materials. Games such as "Where in the World is Carmen San Diego?" are self-directing, but require that students search out information from encyclopedias, almanacs, and dictionaries. Catherine focuses on being a resource for children. She doesn't usually give answers. She gives suggestions about where they might find helpful information. She helps them learn to use the resources.

Now there are more computers, each on its own portable table, too many to bring into the classroom. So, blinds were hung on the windows in the hallway. Three times a week computers are lined up in the hallway outside the door. Six parents are now involved doing different things on the computers.

Some parents do the relatively safe activities like typing and word processing. They assist with the language arts projects. A couple of adventuresome parents try very open activities. Others do educational games or programming with Logo. Logo is a computer language which uses simple commands and allows users to combine patterns to make complex designs. In Logo children can do rather complex graphic programming without having to do much typing. Cooperative learning and peer tutoring happen naturally as children share computer terminals.

Science

Judy Opilowsky and Sherry Smith teamed up a few years ago to develop an extraordinary science center. Judy worked on Mondays, introducing the materials and doing a lab. Sherry followed-up on Tuesdays, doing further exploration and then tying things together with a blackboard recap for the entire class. This system required keeping close track of students and knowing which ones had visited the Science Center the day before. Many topics were covered. The emphasis was on concept development.

In 1986 Haley's Comet was the subject of a major study. Students learned about comets and orbits. They visited an observatory. Children made flip books to show how comets move in orbits and built a model of a comet from dry ice, dust, and Karo syrup. They talked about time, and recurring phenomena, and made time capsules to open during the next passing of Haley's Comet. Children discussed why Haley's Comet could be viewed more easily from some points on the earth's surface than from others. A couple of Charquin grandparents went to Australia to view the comet. Judy went to Arizona. So geography became part of the lesson. The environment is always a major focus in the Science Center. One year conservation was studied with a giant floor map and pretzel power. The map was laid out on the floor. Children were given pretzels. Each pretzel was good for a certain amount of energy. It was decided how many pretzels would be required to move a car, train, bus, or airplane one mile. Children soon learned that two persons who went together could go further with their pretzels than could one person going alone.

The Science Center is an example of how Charquin teaches values. Science Center parents make their perspectives known to the children, while providing students with the opportunity to acquire knowledge and wrestle with issues in their own way. Clearly, the point of the pretzel lesson was that in a world of limited resources we must work together, and that mass transit and ride sharing are responsible solutions. The pretzel experience allowed chidren to figure this out for themselves, and hopefully internalize the lesson for future reference.

Things have changed in the Science Center. Sherry moved on to another center, Land of Blue Sky. Two years later her first child graduated and she left the program. She'll be back when her daughter enters kindergarten. Since Charquin's expansion there are more students, more centers, and less centers time. Not all students have an opportunity to participate in Judy's center every week, so Judy no longer plans a follow-up schedule for individual students. Science lessons are a one shot business, a lab experience with no paperwork.

Shortly after Sherry moved on, Julie Harcos came to Markham as a part-time science prep teacher. Julie enrolled her child in Charquin. She teaches journal keeping in connection with a hands-on based program of experimentation and scientific exploration. Judy and Julie keep in touch so that some lessons can be coordinated.

Judy encourages children to question, test, and come to conclusions about what they experience. Judy likes to encourage children to explore the states of matter. Twice she's helped the children build an ice sculpture. For this project several parents freeze water in containers of different sizes and shapes. Some of the water is colored with food coloring. Judy brings a bag full of snow ice to use for mortar, and the children stick the pieces together. The sculpture sits on the patio. The ice sculpture teaches children about expansion and contraction. Questions such as "Why shouldn't you make ice in a glass container?" must be answered. Children learn about melting and evaporation. They talk about their bodies, and how it feels to work with ice. Even in Hayward's temperate winter weather the structure requires up to two weeks to melt. Every day during the melting process students talk about what is happening. The project is a blending of science and art which is so characteristic of Charquin, where holistic educational philosophy acknowledges the connectedness of disciplines as opposed to their artificial delineations.

While Judy prefers working with concepts rather than themes, she sometimes coordinates Science Center activities with program themes. One theme with which Judy coordinated projects was "Japan." She had students make homemade brushes and ink. It took some experimenting to find something from which to make ink. Berries and strong tea were tried. The children liked painting pictures, but found making the brushes to be the most fun.

A similar idea involved dyeing wool with different natural substances. Yellow onion skins, red cabbage juice, and dandelion leaves were tried. Alum was used to set the colors. The dandelion leaves didn't work. Things don't always go as planned in Judy's center. Even when they don't, something is learned. There's always a lot of questioning and speculating as to what might work next time.

Judy sometimes does what she calls "supermarket chemistry." Toothpaste mixed with cornstarch and glue will dry hard. It makes great sculptures. Soap stones are made by mixing shavings of ivory soap, crayons, and water. The mixture is heated and then cooled. It can be carved. Erasers are made from unflavored gelatin.

At Halloween students want to find ways of making the best fake skin, the ugliest-looking cut, and the best homemade face paint. These projects involve making compounds. Scientific terminology is applied appropriately to whatever the students are doing.

Daryl Berman, another Science Center parent, is a chiropractor. Several times Daryl has done a unit on the human body. He has access to good models and much specific knowledge to share with students. It's an in-depth study that textbook bound science programs can't approach. The study of the body is followed by a study of the five senses. One hearing exercise involves identifying recorded sounds from around the house. The toilet flushing is a favorite. Airplane day is a traditional spring activity, as is kite day. One year Daryl did an airplane project that went on for weeks. The airplane center required little structure and happened all over the floor. Daryl had gotten paper airplane patterns from the Eddie Bauer mail order catalog. The children went crazy for them and made dozens of planes from the various patterns. They tried out each one and finally decided which was the highest flyer and which was the best glider. It was a real study in engineering and aerodynamics. Starting with the children's interest in paper planes, a wide variety of learning took place. The distances flown, heights soared, and tricks performed by planes with various wing designs, nose designs, differing construction materials, etc., were charted. Predictions for future performance were made and tested.

Jeanne Danielsen is a parent who has a large insect collection that she lets students study. She once had the children in the Science Center make butterfly nets. They were going to have their own collections. Another parent objected. The project was viewed as disrespectful to living things and ecologically questionable. While the majority of parents saw nothing wrong with the project, Daryl helped Jeanne find a truly Charquin-like solution. Students caught insects and bugs in their nets, released them into a cage, and Daryl and Jeanne video taped them, and then released them back into the environment.

Land of Blue Sky

In the spring of 1987 Sherry Smith became concerned that a group of fifth graders who came regularly to her Science Center were no longer involved in the activities. They had experienced a good science curriculum and knew a lot of information, but were not making progress. Sherry was casting around for ideas about how she might hook these children. She noted that these students were deeply involved in Dungeons and Dragons-type fantasy play. Everything they wrote had something to do with this theme. Most games had a war-making, dominant-struggle context which seemed inappropriate to Charquin's goals and philosophy.

Sherry looked for a game that would teach science concepts through fantasy play while encouraging children to work together cooperatively

on a constructive task. In the end Sherry and her husband, Harry, teamed up and spent the summer writing their own game, "Land of Blue Sky."

The object of the game is to save the Land of Blue Sky. In the game Charquin students are approached by visitors from the City of Light, an island on the planet of Blue Sky. Scientists there have found that a comet is headed toward their planet, and is expected to destroy it. The task of the players is to help build a laser to blow up the comet. To accomplish this end they must have a dylithium crystal. Nobody knows about the crystal, except that myths say knowledge of how to grow dylithium crystals once existed in the land. The secret is distributed throughout the land, with clues in each of the ten civilizations which comprise the land.

In order to participate in the challenge each player will be teleported up to the City of Light and turned into a character such as, explorer, hunter, etc. Each character is high, middle, or low in each of a number of traits (intelligence, wisdom, dexterity, charisma, strength, etc.). Players work in teams of four to six members, using their team's characters to the best advantage to solve a series of challenges. The tasks stress cooperation and decision-making, and are weighted against strength and fighting.

Land of Blue Sky teaches survival skills. Players must eat and drink daily. They must find water and food in strange environments, and keep an adequate supply with them when they travel. If players fail to do this they develop a "low constitution," and are teleported back to the City of Light and rejuvenated. This interrupts their quest and wastes time. (Since low constitution only happens to someone who is being foolish, no player has yet had this experience.)

As players progress through the Land of Blue Sky they encounter ten races of people. Each race has its own language with a mixed alphabet code. They will encounter traps in the forms of either environmental hazards or characters.

Characters present different types of challenges. Mr. Interpreter will help students understand a new language if they meet his challenge of finding 30 words of more than four syllables. The mermaids will tell a player where to find a helpful hint, if they identify twelve sea shells from Sherry's collection. Sherry makes her field study books available to the students. Costumes are part of the game. On Land of Blue Sky day Sherry and Harry often dress in costume.

There are math challenges and crossword puzzles. With some characters all communications are notes that players must read. One challenge is to "Write a letter to your Mom. Tell her where you are."

Another involves writing a physical description of a character. Other challenges dip into classical mythology.

Judy Opilowsky told me that her favorite challenge tested students' engineering skill by asking them to build a sea-worthy boat in order to pass from one part of the land to another. Sherry provided the materials. Children built their boats. A tub was placed on the patio and filled with water. Boats had to sail across the tub. Sherry's mixer kicked up waves which scuttled poorly designed ships.

P.E.

Charquin's multi-age grouped structure necessitates the selection of P.E. games and activities which children of different ages, sizes, and ability levels can play together. Since Charquin emphasizes cooperation and community building rather than competition, the games chosen and skills emphasized must address these goals.

The Charquin P.E. program has several components. There are traditional afternoon P.E. periods when teachers and parents play games with students and work on specific skills. Throughout the day much P.E. happens spontaneously. Often a parent will do a P.E. Center on the patio. Hula hoops, jump ropes, the balance beam, and tumbling mats may be brought out and supervised by the parent. Parents assist children in mastering physical skills, such as summersaults and head stands. They encourage games which help children develop a feeling for their bodies in space. They teach rhymes and songs that go with various activities.

During recess and break times students bring out the balls and use the backboard for handball. They make up their own games and design rules that enable older and younger children to play together.

While P.E. might sound like a simple matter, there are issues involved. Some children are not athletic, while others play Little League after school. The students who have much physical skill demand competitive physical experiences. If they get their way during a period when everybody has to play they become stars, and some children (as well as their parents) feel put down.

This problem can be handled more easily at Charquin than in traditional classes. There are usually one or two parents who want to involve themselves in competitive athletics. Such parents may have a baseball or soccer center once or twice a week during Centers Time. This gives more athletic students satisfaction without allowing them to skew the program for the entire class. Sometimes P.E. Center parents do skills workshops,

as opposed to games. Like Art Center parents, P.E. parents are an independent lot who value their discipline and find it hard to tell a kid to leave and go to another center when he's having fun. When the classroom starts to look empty, teachers and parents look in Art and P.E. Centers for those kids whom they haven't seen yet this morning. Once or twice a year this issue lands on the Parent Group agenda.

Snack

Snack Time is a long standing Charquin tradition. Each day two families bring a nutritious snack, such as fruit, juice, crackers and cheese. Their children set the snack out just before the end of Centers Time. On sunny days snack is served on the patio. Children take some— if they want to. It's a relaxed time. An emergency stash of food is kept in the classroom for those days when a parent forgets to provide snack. On cooking day the snack comes from the Cooking Center.

A few years ago, some parents who thought snack was just too much trouble tried to convince the Parent Group to discontinue the practice. They lost out. Snack Time is a deeply imbedded tradition. There is an informal coalition between parents and teachers who value the social experience and those who argue the physiological fact that hungry children don't learn. Everyone knows that even in the most attentive of families kids sometimes don't eat breakfast. So, Charquin keeps providing snack.

Experiencing the World - Here and There

Charquin has always placed a priority on teaching children about their community and world. The program promotes a sense of responsibility for the earth and its creatures. Sometimes opportunities to learn about the world are close at hand, or even come to us. Some organizations like the Lawrence Hall of Science or a puppetry group may prepare an assembly for Markham school. One year Charquin invited eight or nine artists to do an Art Fair at Markham. Charquin parents know a lot of interesting people and often invite them to visit the class. In one recent year Charquin's visitors included State Assemblyman Johan Klehs, cartoonist Morrie Turner, Hayward's Mayor, several city council persons, and news anchorwoman Elaine Corral from Channel 2 in Oakland.

Often students must leave the classroom in order to have the desired experiences. Over the years Charquin has become noted as "That program that's always going someplace." Field trips are possible at Charquin

because of the level of parent participation. When schools have no transportation money, taking field trips requires a lot of parents who will drive.

For a number of years Linda Jaster has been Charquin's field trip chairperson. This is a complicated and exhausting job. Linda usually starts her year's planning in the spring by asking parents, teachers, and children which field trips they enjoyed most this year and why they liked them. She also asks participants where they'd like to go next year. Linda then spends her summer investigating various opportunities, writing, calling for information, getting on waiting lists, securing tickets.

Linda keeps the Parent Group, teachers, and Steering Committee informed at each step along the way. She coordinates field trips with monthly themes and expectations for weather, tides, harvests, etc. Linda handles district paperwork, distributes and collects field trip permission slips, and co-ordinates car pools for more than a hundred children and parents.

In a typical year Charquin may go on from ten to fourteen field trips. Some are close to home. Others, such as the yearly camp-out, the nature camp, and trips to San Francisco and Sacramento may be major excursions involving several hours travel time. Charquin's field trips provide rich opportunities for learning about history, nature, living things, and the community. Field trips provide first-hand experience and opportunities to question and learn from docents and specialists from outside the Charquin community.

Lessons From Parents

In the early days the idea that Charquin parents should teach in the classroom offended some people. This concern never made sense to Charquinites. To deny that children can learn significant subject matter from parents is to deny the basic nature of teaching and learning, which is that children learn at any time, in any place, and from any person who gives them the opportunity to explore materials and information about which they care. In other words, learning is meaning driven. To say that only a professional teacher can do this for thirty children five days per week is like saying that only airline pilots may drive on the freeway because they have the best safety record for getting people from one place to another. Such a rule might make us all safer, but we'd all spend a lot of time standing in line, and would go fewer places in the end.

Charquin demonstrates that parents can be good teachers. They teach the child from the day he's born. They know his personality and what draws his attention. They have important gifts and information. They are willing learners of theory and active developers of program. It would be a waste of talent and a perversion of Whole Language philosophy to limit parents to correcting papers, drilling children on their spelling words, and reinforcing instruction. I seriously doubt that many Charquin parents would be participating in the classroom today if those were the rules. People just don't waste their time filling roles that don't challenge and interest them. Perhaps this is the major lesson that the public schools need to learn from Charquin. If we want talented and caring parents to spend their time in the schools we must let them use their talents and do something important.

All of this is not to say that all parents just naturally fall into a good and appropriate role when they enter the program. There is a learning process involved. Sometimes parents enter the program with an "I'm here for my kid" attitude. They might come to class and want to spend all of their time with their own child, to the detriment of both their child and the program. Charquin must turn such attitudes around and help a parent learn to say "I'm here for all the children," and to experience the joy of sharing their interests with a community of learners.

Other parents want to participate in the classroom, but need time to develop their style, focus in on their talents, acquaint themselves with the program, and get to know the children. The community support, adult education, and decision-making apparatus that Charquin provides enables these parents to share their gifts more fully than they might otherwise be able to do.

Multi-age grouping and team-teaching are important structural features for parents. In a traditionally structured school, parents who wish to participate must adjust to a completely new routine, new rules, and a new teacher every year. In such a program teachers have little incentive to invest instructional time helping parents who will move on next year. Charquin's structure offers both support for the parents' experiential learning and a program which allows individual parents and teachers enough time to develop collaborative realationships.

"The Basics"

Charquin agrees with the traditionalists that English, history, foreign language, mathematics, science, the fine arts, and health and physical education are central to a good education. Charquin parts company with the traditionalists by including thinking, feeling, seeing, talking, listening and learning to cooperate in its list of basics. At Charquin children are expected to become powerfully literate and to use language well as a tool for learning and for participating in the community. Consequently, Charquin makes fewer distinctions among disciplines and places more emphasis on the arts than do traditionally structured programs.

Matters of method and evaluation likewise present a contrast between Charquin and more traditional approaches. Charquin's answer to teaching the basics is more complex and holistic than simply putting a good teacher in the classroom, practicing strong discipline and traditional methods, and evaluating the result on a standardized test.

Several years ago a group of parents in a nearby district wanted to start a program like Charquin. Alice Masek and this author were asked to prepare a presentation for their school board. We decided that what the board really wanted to hear was: How do Charquin kids learn to read, write, spell, and compute? Charquin students learn these skills, and the older children test exceedingly well. Still, it was a challenge for us to explain just how Charquin teaches the basics.

We found ourselves fingering through slides and pictures of children writing stories, drawing pictures, listening to a storyteller, rehearsing plays and skits, making scenery and costumes for the plays, reading, working with manipulative materials in the Math Center, going on field trips, and doing a wide variety of activities that looked educational. We were hard pressed to explain just how these activities come together to form a program that produces literate young people.

Of course, we knew that it worked. We had seen it work with our own children, and with many others. The reason for our difficulty was that we were not well read in the research about holistic education.

Over the years Charquin has moved from a basic skills approach to reading, spelling, and math (an approach which employed basal readers, and math and spelling workbooks) toward a Whole Language approach to literacy. Holistic programs, like Charquin, assume that literacy develops naturally, that it is an extension of spoken language. When children become aware of the written word, when they experience the joy and power that its use provides, they quite naturally seek to understand and use it. In their search they go through developmental stages in reading, writing, and math. It is the teachers' responsibility to encourage and enable this process.

The purpose of a Whole Language literacy program is to provide an environment where language is used in all of its richness and power—where children are encouraged to question and to practice literate behavior. The teacher is an opportunist who sees and hears what the child is doing, and suggests approaches designed to help the child answer the questions and solve the problems that he encounters on his way to becoming a literate person.

The Teachers' Role and Development

Shaping Charquin's approach to literacy has been a job for the teachers. It's a job that they've tackled piece by piece. Sometimes they've moved forward. Occasionally, as they've learned and grown, they've moved in other directions, only to retrace their footsteps later. Learning is the major job of Charquin teachers.

In the early years Bob had a skills-based approach to literacy. As the program developed, Bob gained experience and became dissatisfied and bored with basal readers. He began focusing on how children learn, what they told him, and what he wanted to teach them. Bob enrolled in a masters program in Language and Literacy at UC Berkeley, where he found out about Whole Language. As Bob put it, "I felt like Buddha peeking over the wall." (Whitlow, 8)

Bob broke away from the basals. His reading groups became a less central part of his job. He started concentrating on orchestrating literacy events across the curriculum. Bob spent more time helping students research and write reports in social studies and science, produce a newsletter, and perform Readers' Theatre skits. Instead of reading basals, his reading groups often wrote group stories. When they read books, the emphasis was on constructing meaning from what they read, rather than on correcting their miscues and errors of pronunciation.

The focus of the literacy program became one of thinking, reflecting, creating, and communicating. Whether the students were reading, working math problems, writing, spelling a new word, or speaking, they were encouraged to think about what they were doing, to try new things, and to generate ideas and rules.

With Charquin's first expansion, Norma Oden came from Tennyson Parent Nursery to teach the younger children. This was her first experience in teaching reading. Norma knew at the outset that basal readers wouldn't do. But she didn't know where to start.

Like Bob, Norma at first relied on basals. She did a lot of picking and choosing, using mostly the enrichment exercises rather than the standard lessons. Norma supplemented the basal lessons with stories from other sources. She took classes about reading instruction from the McCrackens and classes in cooperative learning and *Math Their Way*. Norma adapted what she learned to her student's needs and developed her own style of teaching.

After several years Norma was a Whole Language teacher. When responding to the controversy over whether McCrackens' methods are really Whole Language, or just creative skills, Norma gives a classic Whole Language answer. "Well, if you do the entire book page by page, it's skills. If you pick and choose and do what the kids need, use other interesting materials, listen to what the kids say, read what they write, and help them use reading as a tool, it's Whole Language."

Parents

As Charquin teachers seek to direct a Whole Language program, they can only go as far and as fast as parents will allow. When parents are in the classroom every day, they have many questions. They also have considerable anxiety. Parent anxiety is reduced when teachers explain the program in terms that parents understand and show them examples of what children are learning. This means that teachers must be very clear about what they are doing and why they are doing it. Parents appreciate art and physical education. What they want to know is how and when their kids are going to learn to read, write, spell, and do math.

When parents become involved in delivering the program, they often become enthusiastic converts. Parents can see how Whole Language supports their families' methods, how it builds on the 'old lap method,' which has long been the mode for parents who want to help their children read. Parents can see for themselves that kids are really learning. When parents participate, doing becomes believing.

Charquin teachers actively encourage parental assistance in carrying out the literacy program. Teachers provide parents with workshops to help them understand and implement Whole Language philosophy in the classroom and at home. Teachers often encourage parents to take special workshops and to share what they have learned with the Parent Group.

The Routines: Sharing the Word

Charquin emphasizes reasoning, feeling, decision-making, and literate behavior. Students of different ages, ability levels, and interests make many decisions for themselves and have many different lessons and experiences throughout the day. This leaves the teachers with the considerable task of providing a focus for the day's activities and pulling things together at crucial points. Around the Rug is the management routine which serves this purpose.

Except on music day (which was described in Chapter 1) Around the Rug is the day's first activity. All children have Around the Rug with their assigned teacher in her home room. At Around the Rug usual administrative tasks such as attendance, announcements, and lunch count, are taken care of by teachers and their student helpers in a most Charquin-like fashion. Nicknames and humorous remarks are employed. Parents and teachers explain the offerings of the day in the various centers. On occasion, a child who wants to staff a center tells about his plans, and invites other children to come to his center. Around the Rug happens several times each day, before lunch, before dismissal, and at any time when a transitional or quieting-down activity seems in order.

Around the Rug is also an important social time. Students and teachers gather and enjoy being part of Charquin. Some parents and younger siblings hang out in the classroom until after the day's first Around the Rug, just for the fun of it. Occasionally a younger sibling accompanies a parent for a day of classroom participation and sits in with the group.

At Charquin all kinds of information is shared. The children participate actively in sharing. Around the Rug cannot be compared to the

"Sharing Time" in traditional classrooms, when five minutes is set aside for the child who has brought something from home and just has to talk. During Around the Rug children may perform a skit, share a joke or a cartoon, or tell intimate tales of family escapades. They talk about the things that make them happy, sad, or angry. A child may relate some new-found scientific truth in terms that are incomprehensible to persons who are uninformed about recent discoveries in science. I once heard a third grade child explain the big bang theory of the creation of the universe in graphic detail. The subject had come up in a discussion at home and he had gone to the library to find out more about it. Newspaper clippings and magazine articles are frequently shared during Around the Rug.

Doing skits during Around the Rug is an old Charquin tradition. The rules for the skits are simple. Skits must have a beginning, a middle, and an end, and they must have been rehearsed before Around the Rug. Often skits take as a theme some issue or conflict which has recently troubled the group. In so doing, they serve as a springboard for further discussion. Happenings on the playground, and who got invited to (or excluded from) what event are often topics of skits. Adults sometimes ask questions, respond to, or expand upon what children share. Occasionally adults will present skits. The skits are much enjoyed and gently critiqued.

During Around the Rug homework is discussed and parent participation in children's learning is reinforced. Homework often takes the form of sponges. A sponge is an assignment with a single question which might be open-ended, or might be a test of logic. Sometimes the question is silly. Other times it's serious. Questions such as: "How many ways can you get to the moon?" encourage creative and fanciful thought. Requests such as: "Name as many kinds of dogs as you can" might call for some research. Sometimes a student's whole family will get involved in a sponge. Creative and funny answers are prized. One sponge that kept parents talking for more than a week went like this: "A man had $100 in the bank. He bought a horse for $50, and sold it again for $60. He bought it again for $70, and sold it for $80. How much money did the man have in the end?"

Around the Rug serves as a stage for sharing the written word and the participants' experiences with language. During Around the Rug teachers spend a lot of time reading to the children. Younger children often sit on the laps of older children or parents. Those of us who were taught in classes where children sat quietly with hands folded on the desk top while the teacher read find it odd to see children drawing, writing, and even cutting pictures from magazines while listening to the story. Parents sometimes ask: "Are they paying any attention?" Surprisingly, when children are questioned about the story line and characters, it is clear that they have understood and are involved in the story.

The Routines: Open-ended Questions

Charquin teachers and parents make a conscious effort to ask open-ended questions which explore reasoning, feelings, opinions, depth of understanding and viewpoint. Bob says that "Asking the right question is one of my greatest challenges and rewards." Open-ended questioning is a basic and pervasive teaching technique, employed energetically and thoughtfully in all of his centers.

When open-ended questioning strategy is used, having the "right answer" is less important than having a "good idea." In traditional classrooms, where teachers more commonly ask questions which focus on recalling facts and content, the children's feelings and reasoning are often ignored. Typical Charquin questions are:

> What's happening here?
> How would you feel if you were in ____'s place?
> If ____ happened instead of what happened in this scene, how would that have changed the ending?
> If you had written this story, how might you have changed it?
> Why?
> How did this story make you feel?

When children respond to these types of questions, their responses often lead to group discussions that expand the lesson or explore ethical issues. This type of thinking takes instructional time. Sometimes other planned activities have to wait. At Charquin thinking takes priority.

The Routines: Sustained Silent Reading

After lunch, every day, Charquin students have a period of sustained silent reading. It's become a ritual. The students don't need to be reminded. They come in, find a book, sit down and read. Allowing class time for independent reading is a way of communicating to students that reading on their own is important. During this time some students read novels and stay with the same book day after day until they finish. Others pick at bits and pieces of informational books or joke books. The student is free to indulge his own interests during silent reading, without adult intervention. It's a time when he is empowered to decide for himself what is important.

The Routines: Unit Planning—Holistic Curriculum Development

Charquin's parent participation format, where each parent staffs his own center, at times leads to a disjointed curriculum. In 1982 Alice Masek noted that there was a lack of coordination in curriculum. Alice suggested that having monthly themes might help. She proposed that units of study could be developed if each parent would agree to plan his center activities around the same theme. The idea was adopted, with some foot dragging. It actually took several years before the group accepted unit planning as an important feature of the program.

As it stands, in the spring of every year students, parents, and teachers are polled about their interests. In June the students vote on a list of themes for the next academic year. Themes such as "Careers," "The Ocean," "The Arts," "Japan," "Transportation" and "The Circus" are typical. Themes are a unifying force in Charquin's planning. Not all centers attend to the themes. Still, field trips, reports, music, art, and social studies generally have enough thematic content to provide a curriculum focus.

The Doors to Literacy: Music and Drama

Charquin views Music, Drama, Art, and Puppetry as basics in the curriculum. Music is central to the Charquin experience. "Don't Fence Me In,"—to which the children have composed their own words—is sung at every See-Ya-Bye (Charquin's year end celebration).

Sometimes music is coordinated with the month's curriculum theme. Alice Masek, who first encouraged Charquin to adopt monthly themes, has led Charquin singing for over ten years. Once when the monthly theme was Australia, Alice helped children learn songs from Australia. They later took a field trip to the Australian Consulate in San Francisco. Songs from this unit are now part of the *Charquin Songbook*.

Several years ago Alice taught the children songs from "Peter Pan." Bob read Peter Pan in its original version. The story gave much opportunity for discussing history, language, prejudices, and sex role stereotypes. The children wrote their own script and improvised freely. They projected their voices and the personalities of the characters. The performance was dynamic.

Peter Pan brought together the talents of many parents and children. It took over a month to prepare the play. Scenery was built in the Art Center. Sewing Center moms enlisted the assistance of other parents to make costumes. Peter Pan was music, art, drama, and literacy rolled into one. The performance was presented at See-Ya-Bye to an appreciative audience.

Alice Benjamin works in Charquin's music program. In her other life Alice is a professional musician with the San Jose Symphony. Alice B. explains her mission as that of exposing children to the best music ever written while they are still in elementary school. She does music appreciation with the children once a week. Alice brings professional musicians to class. They share their instruments and talents with children. On Mozart's birthday Alice brought in a fellow musician from the San Jose Symphony who impersonates Mozart. He made a real hit as he told the children about Mozart's life in the first person.

Students do some singing with Alice B. They perform music written during all periods, from the renaissance through modern times. They do simple part singing and learn to read notation. They also do instrumental work which is geared to two different groups, those who take lessons or participate in Markham's instrumental program and those who do not. For students with more music background Alice has started a Charquin orchestra. Students with less musical training do activities such as performing the percussion parts to Haydn's "Toy Symphony." Students present a monthly concert for their Charquin schoolmates.

Susan Rockwell, a parent who says her "passion is Shakespeare," joined Charquin in 1984. Susan's first major project was directing a performance of excerpts from *A Midsummer-Night's Dream*. Five and six year olds enjoyed performing the challenging lines along with fifth graders. The students performed for the Markham School student body.

For Halloween in 1988 all of the children participated in performing selections from *Macbeth*. Children who dropped the cow eyes, raw liver, beef hearts, and other assorted entrails into the witches' cauldron, will never forget *Macbeth*.

Performing *Macbeth* for Halloween is now a Charquin tradition. Charquin students have also performed portions of *Hamlet, Twelfth Night, Romeo and Juliet, Richard III,* and *King Lear.*

Shakespeare is performed in various settings, in the classroom, in Markham's multi-purpose room, and on an outdoor stage that parents built on the patio. Shakespeare productions attract a great deal of parent participation. Many parents take time out to come to school for the performances, helping with make-up, adding the forgotten touch to the costume, or just enjoying the performance.

Charquin children enjoy performing—dressing up in costumes, making up their faces, designing scenery, learning lines, and improvising. These are powerful experiences that give students prestige within the community. Vocabulary, history, and information that would never be understood in other classrooms are part of the Charquin experience.

Linda Cano tells me that when her son, Travis, was in kindergarten, he played a word game with his grandmother. Travis suggested the word 'cauldron.'

"What's a cauldron?" Grandma asked.

Travis replied, "You know, it's a big pot, like the one the witches used in *Macbeth*."

Grandma was convinced that Travis was a genius.

But learning to play the cultural trivia game and getting good strokes from others are not the only advantages that students get from performing. Performing helps children sharpen their oral reading and speaking skills. Performing helps children bring meaning to and take meaning from the written word. In other words, performing helps children become literate individuals.

The Doors to Literacy: Puppetry

Several years ago Mary Brito developed the Puppetry Center. At first she worked with whatever materials were at hand. Soon Mary wanted better equipment. She wrote a successful proposal for a mini grant to purchase materials for her project. With the grant funds, Mary had a portable theater built. She purchased some lovely puppets and brought a troupe of professional puppeteers to Markham School for an assembly. The puppeteers spent the day working in the classroom.

Mary helped children make puppets and props and perform plays of all descriptions. Punch and Judy was a favorite. Mary encouraged students to improvise and helped them to learn their lines and make decisions about how things would work.

The Doors to Literacy: Readers' Theater

Mary also worked with Readers' Theater. This project requires that children read a play through several times, find a few simple props, and then perform the play with script in hand. Mary often chose plays that had African or Asian roots. Many Charquin second graders and even some of the first graders are capable of performing Readers' Theater. It is a powerful literacy experience.

Several times a year a couple of children get together and decide to be playwrights. Mary encourages this activity. The two Justins started the tradition of Charquin playwrights when they were both in the third grade. The Justins collaborated in writing a play about a Charquin child getting ready to catch his morning car pool ride. Their friends served as actors. This project demonstrated a considerable level of sophistication about how plays are written and designed as well as a high level of writing ability. The audience related to the theme and made the writers instant stars. Since then a number of Charquin children have written plays for the stage. These plays are performed. The scripts are bound, displayed, and saved for later use.

Performance experiences provide Charquin children with opportunities to develop self-esteem, confidence, language, and literacy. Performance also encourages listening skills. One of the most heartening facts of life at Charquin is that the children really listen to each other.

Writing

Writing is central to Charquin's literacy program. Charquinites, like many other children, come to school with a great desire to write. They often know how to write their names. They sometimes copy printed letters from cereal boxes and picture books. Charquin capitalizes on their interest.

Charquin's classroom routines and the centers that parents develop involve children in many types of writing. All Charquin children spend ten minutes a day writing in their journals. Older children are journal partners with five and six year olds. Fast friendships blossom between journal partners as children share their experiences.

Every day in Norma's room a couple of centers are devoted to writing activities for younger children. A center typically has one parent and four or five children in attendance at any given time. The centers are flexibly handled so that as one child leaves another child can take his place. Centers don't present writing lessons. They present writing opportunities.

One parent might be helping children write Halloween stories, or stories about a recent event or field trip. At the same time another group of children, assisted by a parent, may be writing letters to companies and government agencies which give away free sample merchandise. In one project students wrote letters requesting free samples from companies. The project went on for several months. Children wrote one letter after another to companies that gave away seeds, posters, and doodads of one kind or another. When a child received something in the mail at home he brought it to school to share. Often the child then wrote another letter to another company.

Writing: Writers' Workshop

A few summers ago Bob took a class from the Bay Area Writing Project. The Project is based on the work of Donald Graves, Lucy Calkins, and Susan Sowers (Graves, 1983). Bob was impressed with the idea of helping children to cooperate in their writing, of encouraging them to see writing as a process which is carried out within a community of writers — a Writers' Workshop. Alice Masek, a parent who was deeply involved in her own writing, took a Writers' Workshop training session from the Hayward Unified Schools. Later other parents took similar classes.

Charquin students who are independent writers participate in Writers' Workshop. This involves roughly half of the second graders and all of the older children. The workshop meets for one hour and fifteen minutes four mornings per week. Sixteen students of similar age and ability rotate through the program every two weeks. Each student keeps a Writers' Workshop folder. Parents get involved as writers, listeners, and critics.

Writers' Workshop requires teachers to model expected writing behaviors for students. This means that teachers write while the students write. Teachers also share their writing on occasion. There are five basic steps in the Writers' Workshop programs:

1. Pre-writing activities:

These activities might include brainstorming descriptive words or sharing anecdotes with a friend. One pre-writing activity involved writing a list of words or short expressions which reminded the writer of an anecdote from his past. Bob set the stage by writing a list which included "Mud in the orange grove," "Cherry bombs over Arrowhead," "Tree house," etc. Then students asked him to tell the anecdote behind the expressions which interested them. After Bob had told his anecdote he asked each student to write a list of expressions and meet with three friends in their group. The students in the group took turns telling the anecdotes which interested their friends.

2. Free writing:

Once students have completed their pre-writing activity they must write about one of the anecdotes that they told. Each day when students arrive in the Writers' Workshop they do twenty minutes of free writing. The teacher models the expected activity by writing with them. During this time mechanics and neatness are ignored. Creative spelling and structure is encouraged. As Bob puts it, "The five sentence paragraph is dead." The goal at this time is simply to get words on paper.

3. Response groups:

During this time students meet again with the groups with which they worked during the pre-writing activities. They read their work and ask for the response of the group. Students may either make a positive comment, or ask a question. No negative comments are permitted. This is a support group.

4. Re-write:

When the students have heard the comments of the response group they re-write their work. They may choose either to answer their group's questions or not to answer them. Students are instructed to "show, don't tell." Use of descriptive words and dialogue are emphasized.

Again the teacher models what is expected. On the overhead projector he lets students know that sloppy is o.k. and spelling is still unimportant. At this stage the ideas are the primary concern. In their re-write students circle those words about which they have a question.

It should be noted that not everything a student writes is selected for a re-write. Students write new material every day. They only re-write the material that they like.

5. More Responding:

The re-write is taken back to the response group where it is read and responded to again. An adult is allowed to read the paper. The rules for adults are the same as the rules for students. No negative comments are allowed—positive comments or questions only. The adult may correct only those words that are circled. (This takes tremendous restraint. Students learn a little at a time without being discouraged by a paper covered with red ink.)

6. Final Draft—maybe:

If the student is satisfied with his work he may produce a final draft. If he has entered his re-write on the computer, as some students do, this is an easy task. Because "writing is an agreement between the writer and the reader," the work is read in front of all sixteen students. Questions are asked about process. "How did this story change between the first and last draft? Why did you say___the way that you did?" These questions help the child to reflect on his learning and skills.

The paper is then posted in the hall for all to enjoy. (Parents also enjoy reading students' work when they arrive early for car pooling.) When the work is removed from the display it is placed in the child's workshop folder. At the end of the year each child is asked to select one piece, his best writing from all that was done this year. This work is published in a bound volume. Each child gets a copy.

Writers' Workshop seeks to encourage fluent, descriptive, thoughtful writing. The ownership that the student feels as a consequence of choosing her own topics and the social support that she receives from working in a community of writers keeps the student going and growing through tough times. This sample written by a fifth grader and published in Charquin's 1989 book gives a taste of the kind of student writing that the program inspires.

Adriel's Dream
by Adriel Brito

Once this kid named Adriel decided to invite his best friend
to spend the night. His name was Chad. When Chad got to
Adriel's house, they had a pillow fight, ate jelly beans, and
pulled frogs apart. By this time they were so exhausted
their tongues were hanging out like dogs. When they got
home Nathan (Adriel's big brother) was bitching at his
mom. Adriel decided to have some fun, so he copied
everything his brother said like a baby pig. Nathan pounced
on Adriel like a panther and soon they were grappling and
rolling on the ground.

"Nathan, you stop hitting your brother!"

"But, Mom."

"No buts, go to your room!"

After eating quesadillas for dinner Adriel and Chad watched T.V. for a few hours and then they went to bed. They woke up and went outside to see the extravagant sunrise. They were very rudely interrupted to see an old thing walk up the street.

"Hi," said Chad.

Little did they know their lives were in danger. The zombie turned, they swallowed their Adam's apples, and their hearts skipped a beat because the zombie had maggot—filled eyes and bloody flesh hung from its face.

Then, to Adriel's horror, it pointed a boney finger at him and said, "You die."

Adriel's knees got weak. He tried to run but found himself at the zombie's knee. It brought an axe down on his neck. It was 2 a.m. in the morning, just a dream.

Writing: Report Writing

For many years report writing was a regular monthly activity at Charquin. All children wrote reports, even kindergartners, who might only be able to draw a picture about the topic and tell the class about it. Reports were written and then presented orally. Report writing involved parents. The standing joke was, "Well, at least I've learned how to write a report since my kid started Charquin."

In Charquin's early days Bob required students to write reports for two reasons. First, report writing served the instructional purpose of enabling the teacher to evaluate whether students were capable of putting together, organizing, and communicating information. In an open program where students moved around a lot and had many sources of information, Bob found it difficult to assess the students' development unless he saw a major piece of work periodically. The second function served by report writing was that it presented parents with an invitation to become involved in a writing experience with their children.

Today report writing no longer serves as the major vehicle for assessing student progress in writing, since Writer's Workshop activities also provide this sort of information. Report writing often starts as late as

February. These days kindergartners and first graders usually don't write reports. Report writing now involves more cooperative group effort. While students still do individual reports, they most often work together with three or four other students, sharing their research and the tasks of writing and illustrating. As before, children choose their own topics, based on the monthly theme. They produce beautiful work and display it in the hallway gallery.

When Dana did the last report of her Charquin career her topic was "Hair Accessories." She had researched what women have worn in their hair over the last two hundred years in Europe and America. Dana located similar items and made various types of bows and ornaments from materials that she purchased or scrounged from the sewing box. The students enjoyed the report and asked many questions.

Spelling

As often happens with Charquin, one change leads to another. When Charquin teachers and parents decided to try a process-oriented literacy program, the old practice of teaching spelling from lists of words no longer fit. Children are now encouraged to think about how to spell words, to give it a try, to be creative, and not to stop writing because they can't spell a word. This approach to spelling allows children to build fluency in writing. It means that first graders can write expressively long before they can spell correctly—that they can do what writers do: they can communicate.

So, how does the Charquin child learn to spell? According to Donald Graves (1983,184-94), the child learns to spell as he uses his ear to decide how to represent the various words that he wants to write. Richard Gentry (16-20) expands upon the process when he says, "Kids learn to spell by inventing spelling ...Spelling is a constructive developmental process." At first the child is a "spelling babbler." He uses alphabet symbols to represent words, the way a baby uses sounds. The child who writes a lot progresses to semi-phonetic spelling, then to phonetic spelling, and later to mature spelling. Graves and Gentry agree that encouraging children to do a great deal of purposive writing and to invent spellings helps them move through the developmental process and become better spellers.

Graves and Gentry both note that some children have more difficulty with spelling than do others. For many children good spelling is a gift. All three Charquin teachers have noted this. They struggle with finding ways to help older children—those for whom conventional spelling does not come naturally—become better spellers. Children are encouraged to use all of the resources at their disposal, the environment, their friends, the dictionary, and a spelling list of frequently used words. They keep writing and working at it.

Still, teachers talk about making a list of some rules that will help. If they do, it will be a short list. Gentry (31) suggests that there are only about six rules that are helpful. He also suggests that for children who are spelling at the phonetic and transitional developmental levels, that there is some merit in beginning a formal study of spelling. (This stage is most often accomplished during second grade.) Gentry notes that the Fitzgerald Method, and the Horn Method, together with some phonics, might be helpful to children. But he cautions that "(t)he real foundation for spelling is frequent writing." Traditional methods of memorizing lists, and rules, and copying the misspelled word numerous times, do not seem to help.

Math - Thinking, Cooperating, and Doing

In the early days of Charquin, the math program was individualized. Each child went to a Math Center during Centers Time and worked, more or less individually, with the Math Center parent. (Working with a friend was o.k., but it didn't happen often.) This arrangement was not satisfying to parents and teachers. As might be expected, there were a few motivated boys who went to the Math Center daily and zipped through several workbooks a year. Many other students treated Math Center as a necessary evil, to be avoided as often as possible.

The math program began moving in a new direction when Bob took classes at the Bay Area Math Project. That's where he met Mary Laycock. Mary is a math consultant who specializes in using manipulative materials to develop children's mathematical thinking ability.

When Mary's granddaughter was enrolled in Charquin, Mary volunteered to help out with math. All kinds of creative things started happening in the Math Center. Children built cubes and pyramids out of construction paper and tested to see how many pyramids fit inside a cube and what types of structures could be built with pyramids. Children were taught to use unit cubes for adding, subtracting, multiplying, and dividing. Design blocks and colorful transparent fraction tiles were used to discover geometric and numeric principles. A supply of appropriate equipment was collected and neatly stored on wheel carts in all of the classrooms. The materials were used for counting, sorting, design-making, and the solving of complex problems. For K—2nd graders math manipulatives (M&Ms)

are still a routine part of the Charquin program. Older children are also encouraged to use manipulatives when tackling challenging concepts. Charquin's math program encourages children to think, generalize, and find different ways of approaching problems. Children often spend considerable time exploring geometric patterns and designs. At Charquin, girls enjoy math (which is unusual in today's youth culture). And, the book doesn't set the upper limit for what children can do. I once observed a group of first and second graders and was surprised to find that they could use Unifix Cubes to solve problems of repeated addition—in other words, they could multiply, although they didn't call it multiplication. More tradition-bound classrooms usually reserve such problems for third graders.

Charquin teachers and parents seek to integrate math instruction into all areas of the curriculum. Gardening and science are subjects where math concepts are integrated into discussions of recurring phenomena and record keeping. The cooking program gives a fine example of the type of integration which takes place. Making Stone Soup is a cooking, literacy, and graphing experience. On Stone Soup Day the story "Stone Soup" is read. Children are encouraged to bring vegetables from home for the soup. The vegetables are placed on a large grid on the floor in the center of the room. One column for the potatoes, one for the onions, one for carrots, and so forth. Teachers and children take turns creating and naming new categories. After all of the vegetables are sorted and counted, a graph is made on the board. Then the vegetables are cut up for the soup.

Charquin's math program for older children differs from the program for younger children. Younger children do most of their math activities in centers, under the supervision of parents. "Math Their Way" is the primary source book. It contains many M&Ms type activities. This program involves a great deal of counting, sorting, categorizing, block-building, and design-making. Older children do math in cooperative learning groups. Fifth and sixth graders do 'book math' with Karen a couple of times a week. The point of book math is to teach children who have never used a math book how to use it as a resource. Also, they do some practice on algorithms. These skills will be important in middle school.

Menu

Menu is a cooperative learning, process-oriented management system which is employed in the older children's math program and occasionally in language arts. A few years ago when Dr. Ruth Parker was the math specialist with Alameda County Schools and her daughter enrolled in Charquin, Ruth introduced Menu to the teachers and Parent Group. During Menu children are selected and placed in groups of two, three, or four. Sometimes grouping is done by a simple drawing of cards. Other times teachers or the students themselves may decide who works with whom. After students are placed in groups they work on Menu tasks. Some of the tasks are done individually; some can be shared with a partner or done by the whole group. These tasks are usually challenging and open-ended, having multiple solutions. They draw on the children's creativity and keep them interested. It's not like doing a page out of the book. Drill is avoided. Cooperation is encouraged. The Menu for the week is displayed on Menu cards which are hung in a conspicuous place in the classroom.

During Menu Time each group of students works at its own pace on the assigned tasks for the time allotted. Manipulative materials, such as unit blocks, Unifix cubes, and peg boards are always available for students who want to try out a theory. Groups may approach the task cards in any order that suits their fancy. Each of the students keeps his own Menu notebook, or journal. The students are aware that they must finish the required tasks in the time allotted or meet again during free time to finish.

When a group finishes a task card each member of that group must write in her journal not only the problems and answers, but a short reflective statement about the process she pursued in getting the answers. Such statements may include a report of what didn't work and why it didn't work as well as what did work. For the group that finishes all of the tasks there may be a dessert card. Dessert is not just extra work of the same type. It's a task which is appealing and requires more advanced skills than the other lessons.

After all groups have finished their week's menu, they meet Around the Rug for a de-briefing. Each group has a spokesperson who shares the results. Explaining their work is crucial. While experiential learning makes it easier for children to internalize concepts, the concept really isn't assimilated until it can be verbally encoded. When children explain math concepts to their classmates they sometimes draw diagrams and project them on the over-head projector. Their explanations are often amazingly mature. If things get exciting or controversial, as they often do, children other than the leaders join in to share the discussion and present their ideas.

Since the tasks are open-ended there are frequently many ideas to be shared. Alternative techniques for arriving at the same solutions are explored by the group. Typical questions asked during de-briefing are: If I do this, will that always happen? Why? Why not? How many different ways can you find to get that answer? Questions such as these keep children thinking. They develop concepts and motivate children to use math as a means of finding solutions, hypothesizing, and testing. Occasionally an incorrect response is shared. Sometimes more than one group makes the same mistake. When differences of opinion or fact surface it is an honor to be the one who can explain the error and provide a correct solution. During Menu time mistakes always belong to the group. No individual is allowed to be embarrassed by taking the fall alone. On the other hand, the student who does a good job of explaining a particularly elegant solution is thoroughly appreciated.

At Charquin, cheating is carefully defined to help students and parents see the distinction between cheating and cooperating. Helping the other person to learn is cooperating. Cheating means giving the other person the answer without helping him learn. Cooperating is encouraged. Cheating is not. When groups work cooperatively, all members of the group must understand and be able to do the lesson in order for the group to reach its goal. For this reason children must learn both the information, and how to teach and explain it to their friends. They must practice respectful attitudes and learn helpful methods of giving feedback to group members. Students must also develop skill in keeping their group focused.

Reading Groups

Probably in no other program description could I have gotten this far without discussing reading groups. Yes, Charquin has reading groups. As in most classrooms, teachers have traditionally spent much of their morning instructional time teaching reading. As I said earlier, teachers have attempted to de-emphasize reading groups in favor of orchestrating literacy events across the curriculum. Bob has been most successful in doing this with the older children. Nevertheless, reading groups still happen for both older and younger children.

The groups generally consist of from three to six children who meet with teachers during Centers Time. Younger children are grouped more by who works well together than by achievement levels. For older children, groups tend to be formed more according to achievement levels, although how well students work together is still a consideration. Grouping is generally more flexible than in traditional classrooms and more often takes the interests and feelings of students into account. Since the groups aren't plodding through a packaged text lock-step, there is the opportunity to bring a student into a particular group for a few days in order to do a special activity that relates to his interest. Groups don't remain fixed and they are multi-age grouped. The children's own experiences and interests are central to the reading program. In one series of lessons the younger children wrote stories about the beach. It was the first week of November. Charquin had just returned from its annual trip to the pumpkin patch and the beach. The theme for the month was "Oceans."

Norma wrote the words "At the beach I saw a—" on a card and put the card on the story chart. Each child told what he saw. "Sea Lion," Mussel," "Hermit Crab," etc. The child's own word was written on a card. He drew a picture of the word, and then placed the card on the chart. The chart became a record of the group's experience.

Each child then wrote his own story and drew a picture of it. They read their stories to the group and added the new word to their vocabulary ring. Each child's story was displayed in the classroom or hallway and then added to her writing journal.

During the next couple of weeks, Roxanne, an Art Center parent, involved students in drawing murals about the beach and stuffing large paper fish of many types. The hallway display showed how unit planning comes together around themes which support the literacy program.

In Norma's reading group the children's own stories and writing are supplemented with a wide variety of stories and nursery rhymes, some of which are in a Big Book. Norma makes a wide variety of books available to students. These books range from bound copies of the students' writing to comic books, novels, and encyclopedias. Reading groups are fun. They usually meet in a sunny corner of the room around the table. Groups are small; four or five students. Charquin teachers enjoy the process and work supportively with students. They don't push a time frame.

With older students the content is more advanced. Basal readers are seldom used unless they happen to have an interesting story or a lesson which addresses an immediate need of the students. The content includes high interest, age-appropriate fiction, biographies, poetry, and literature of all types. Sometimes the activity might involve preparation for a social

studies or science lesson. Other times groups meet in the library to do research. Students generally select their own topics.

Bob often structures his reading groups with a directed activity which requires students to think and predict. Bob activates thought and motivation by asking open-ended questions. Such questions as: "What do you think will happen next?" and, "Why do you think so?" stimulate creative thought processes. When the students read they are reading to find out whether they were correct. They're not reading to answer the teacher's question. Bob doesn't let the students know whether their predictions are correct. He sets a casual and supportive tone and avoids putting students on the spot.

Thinking and constructing meaning—real reading—is the point of the process. Mechanics and word attack skills are taught only when students show a need for them. Sometimes Bob asks a few factual questions at the end of a story just to monitor basic student understanding and reading competency.

Unity of Purpose - Social Studies

The various components of Charquin's literacy program are thoroughly mixed and over-lapped but each addresses a specific need in the child's search for literacy. Around the Rug is a time for reading literature, sharing ideas, practicing spoken language, and expanding the child's cultural understanding. Performance opportunities reinforce these skills and understandings. Writers' Workshop promotes the writing process. Most language skills are learned within the context of the writing experience, with an occasional Language Menu exercise to encourage new directions. Sustained silent reading encourages children to read independently. Math presents challenges, develops concepts, stimulates problem-solving and thinking. Math, reading, and writing are tools that children use to extend and to express both what they know, and what they are learning.

In order for the components to hang together, forming a holistic program which involves parents and produces literate and caring students, there must be a focus which goes beyond the acquisition of skills into the world of ideas and understanding. As Bob says, "Ideally the anchor of the curriculum is social studies."

Because social studies is by definition interdisciplinary and concerned with the study of social relationships and the functioning of society, it presents an excellent opportunity for applying and reflecting upon information gained from other sources, such as the learning centers. This only works if social studies is presented in an organized way by a person who is present every day, someone who has an over-view of what is happening program-wide. At Charquin the teachers do it. Social Studies usually happens in the afternoon, after the kindergartners go home.

Charquin's third through sixth graders are heavily involved in Social Studies. Concepts and values are the core of the Social Studies curriculum. Skills of inquiry and respect for the diversity of the human race are encouraged. The central questions of history (Who are we? Where do we come from? and What does this mean to us now?) are dealt with both seriously and playfully as students explore the possibilities. The intent is that students will develop a sense of their own connectedness and a sensitivity to the common elements in the human experience as well as to those experiences and beliefs which make people different. It is hoped that students will learn to see their destiny as one that is shared with others, past and present.

While seeking to involve children in the search for meaning and connectedness Bob often draws upon his background in religious studies. Such inquiry is made very special at Charquin where students are a diverse group. Within the Charquin family there are Native Americans, a Hindu family from India, Protestants, Catholics, Jews, and an assortment of persons who have not adopted religious labels. While bringing religion into the classroom is unusual in the Public Schools, Bob does it. He involves parents from different cultural and religious backgrounds in his presentations and discusses not only what different people in different places believe, but how their beliefs shape the ways in which they live. His evenhanded and respectful handling of the topic makes the appropriateness of such materials unquestionable.

Since ideas and concepts are the focus of Social Studies, almost any period, locality, or people will do as a subject of inquiry. On one occasion there was a unit on Africa. Students did reports about different parts of Africa, the geography, people, religions, economics, etc.

Map-making is an important element in the Charquin social studies curriculum. Starting in about the third grade students are taught about scale and grids. They are shown how to look at the portion of the map which is in one square on the grid, and enlarge it by making it fit a larger square on a larger grid. They go on to do the same on the next square, and the next, until the map is complete.

Every year the older children do a major map-making project. This project involves creating a map of a large area, a continent, or a country. They prepare for the project by drawing several small maps. The major project involves drawing a map on a piece of cardboard and applying a salt and flour dough to show the geographical features. When the dough is dry the students paint these features and the political boundaries. The maps require more than a week for completion. During the unit on Africa each child made a salt and flour map of the African continent. The project provided much opportunity to discuss natural boundaries, political boundaries, climate, how things fit together, and how people survive on this planet.

Once a year the older children, with the help of one or two parents, draw a giant map on the asphalt outside. It is painted in tempera, so that it will need to be done again the next year. (Doing it is the fun part.) Students draw the grid. Then they chalk the lines. Masking tape is placed on each side of the lines, and paint is applied between the pieces of tape. When the paint is dry the tape is removed and the map is complete.

The younger children sometimes use the map as a play space—making up their own games as they go along. In one such game a player stands on a state and calls out its name. The second player determines whether the name called out is the correct name for the state. If it isn't, a correction is suggested. The first player jumps from one state to another, and then into the ocean—stopping only when both players agree that a mistake has been made.

One Social Studies unit focused on the colonial period. Students formed role playing teams and developed plays about starting a colony in the New World. Such questions as: How will we get there? How long will it take? Where will we locate the settlement? What must we take with us? Who will go? How many people will be in the party? and, How will we treat the natives? had to be answered by each team.

Along with the role playing there was considerable research done by students and materials provided by teachers and parents. These resources put students in contact with how the story was played out historically. The fact that settlers destroyed native cultures was pointed out—as was the fact that such destruction is still going on in the world today. Questions like: How do we relate to that? What can be done? were asked—not so much because answers are demanded, as because asking questions and searching for meaning are central to learning.

Since Charquin is in California there has been a traditional emphasis on California History. Native Americans, the Gold Rush, and railroads are all subjects of study. Historical sites are close at hand. Visiting the sites builds the sense of connectedness. During a camping trip in the gold country children did role playing games about miners and settlers based on research they gathered beforehand. In different years excursions to the State Capitol Museum, the Railroad Museum, and the Ohlone Indian shell mounds on San Francisco Bay are included in this unit. Once again, music is brought in and songs are learned. Math, as used by miners and store owners, is explored. Cooking, art, sewing, and handicrafts are discussed, and tried out. Reports are written. The exploits, both worthy and immoral, of historical figures are discussed. The motivations of people for doing what they did, be it starting new homes in the West, ripping off the miners, or exploiting Chinese laborers, are explored and discussed.

Such discussions lead quite naturally to an exploration of how and by whom laws are made and what can be done by individuals when the process is unfair. A visit by our State Assemblyman and the field trip to Sacramento to visit with him gave students contact with a legislator. Other politicians have visited the classroom, including the Mayor and several City Council persons.

Reading the books, meeting the people, and seeing the buildings, structures, and icons are what people commonly think of as social studies. It's learning about the nation and its government. But all of this stops somewhat short of involving children directly in participatory democracy.

At Charquin the experience must go further. Not only do students write letters to legislators, but when situations arise that impact the lives of children, they are encouraged to get involved. One example of this involvement centered on the State's plan to build a freeway through Hayward, cutting off a piece of the school's playground and making the environment noisy and dirty. Some of the children participated in an informational walk through town and a rally which followed the walk. At the rally they helped "Paint the City."

Students wrote letters to the Mayor, (now former Mayor) whom they knew to be a supporter of the freeway project. The Mayor complained to the Superintendent and then to the newspaper. He said that the children were involving themselves in matters beyond their years. (Imagine the power that a child feels when they get under the mayor's skin just by writing a letter!) The older children each wrote a letter to the Editor of the newspaper. Unfortunately, the newspaper did not print their letters,

Dear Editor,

I am a student at Markham school. I think that kids have rights to express there feelings too. I am old enough to understand and believe in how I feel. I don't want a free-way in the back of my school. But why can't I tell that to the mayor. I was really offended when the mayor thought we were too young to write letters to him. I respect his opinion but I wish he would respect mine.

Sincerlly,
Dana M. Cano
Age 11 six grade

choosing to print several from adults instead. Still, I was struck by the brilliance of the letters, when compared to the silly letters they had written on other subjects over the past several years. It was clear that this activity had really involved the children. Each and every letter made an important point. The freeway has not yet been built and whether it will be is in doubt. The Social Studies program is centered on education for empowerment in a democratic society. While this is often assumed to be a liberal agenda, political activity is never presented in a partisan way. In fact, both major political parties are represented within the Charquin faculty, and parents are likewise a diverse group.

The traditional approach to Social Studies (which quickly puts most students to sleep) is to start a unit by reading the text. Since the focus at Charquin is on inquiry rather than pouring in facts, it is necessary to find out what students know and to structure questions which provide for useful reflection.

Bob employs a simple, old fashioned technique to find out what students know. He asks them, "What do you know about this?" He writes everything they say on a big chart. He doesn't correct their errors yet.

At the end of the project, after every student has done his research and presented his report, the class is asked, "What did we learn in this unit?" The two lists are one of the assessment tools by which the success of the program is measured. When the second list shows that new concepts have been developed and more command of the facts is present, the unit was successful and the children have learned. The projects and reports that the children produce are also viewed as tools for assessment. This may sound overly simple, but when children produce work which demonstrates the acquisition and application of knowledge, that work is a more important tool for assessment than any test that the State could devise.

Even for traditional teachers, social studies is the subject that is most likely to lead to field trips and fun. Kids live in a go-and-do-it world. Experience makes what has been taught and discussed real in the lives of children. But taking children on field trips and introducing them to lots of people and artifacts, as Charquin does, doesn't insure that they will put the information together and use it well. Reflected experience is what teaches. Reflection happens when the right questions are asked at the right time. Seeing that this happens is the central planning issue for the social studies teacher. Children realize their significance, power, and responsibility as citizens of this nation and world when enriching experiences are given meaning through reflection and group discussion.

Summary

Charquin defines literacy broadly to include more than the skills of reading, writing and computing. A literate person is defined as one who has a broad base of knowledge and the skill to express himself and explore new ideas in many different areas of inquiry. This definition has made it necessary to re-think the basics and cast them in a broader light, with art, music, science and opportunities for social learning near the center of the curriculum. The daily routines, instructional methods, and curriculum are consciously designed to move the student toward a powerful literacy.

The School Environment

A major challenge for teachers is that of ordering the environment so that educational objectives can be attained. Children must function in an environment that gives them clear messages with regard to what is expected if they are to learn those things which are valued by their teachers, parents, and the society at large. In most classrooms—where following directions and finding correct answers are the value—much of this structuring is dictated by the system, its bells, routines, textbooks, and equipment. Charquin presents an alternative environment.

Classroom Order

Traditional teacher-dominated classrooms which focus on academic skills instruction and often define those skills narrowly present one type of order. This order gives the student a minimum number of choices and little access to materials and resources outside of those contained in his own desk. The teacher controls both the content of instruction and the materials for learning.

Quite another environmental order is presented by Charquin. Over the years, some observers and even an occasional parent have characterized the Charquin classroom as disorganized, even trashy. And, at times, it has been. Part of the perception of disorder was, and is, in the eyes of the beholder. People who are used to seeing traditional classrooms and lack understanding for the objectives of the program just don't understand what they're seeing. At Charquin the observer sees process, not the endpoint. The environment is an ongoing experiment. The organizational difference between Charquin and other classrooms is similar to the difference between the bedroom of the child who cleans his own room, and the bedroom of the child whose mother does the job for him. The first bedroom is not as neat, but it's clear both to whom it belongs and that the youngster is learning something through the experience.

At Charquin the program belongs to the parents and kids. It's not the teacher's job to keep up the environment. (Although they spend considerable time doing just that.) Maintaining order is a group project. Since not all adults are that much neater than kids, the business of putting things away and cleaning up is a frequent issue at Parent Group meetings and a social learning experience for everybody.

The reasons for Charquin's organizational scheme go beyond problems of perception and ownership. The environment is intentional. Charquin's organization supports the broader academic and social objectives of the program. Since Charquin students and parents are expected to take responsibility for their own learning and to be active participants in the teaching/learning process, the environment must allow them to explore. As compared to students and parent participants in other classrooms, Charquin members are granted both more freedom to move and to talk among themselves, and more access to materials. Likewise, Charquin's schedule allows participants to make more choices, and permits them more time for exploration and self-discovery.

Desks, Cubbies and Coats

Over the years children have answered the question, "What's different about Charquin?" by saying "We don't have desks." This may seem superficial, but to the children the statement carries content. Once Charquin was displaced from its classrooms for several days by a painting crew. The children gathered their things and moved to a room in another wing were they spent three days pretending to be a regular class. Staying in their seats was a big issue. The students were glad to get back to Charquin.

Charquin students have no desks. So they put their personal belongings in cubbies. In the old days a large homemade structure with a big cubby for each child sat near Charquin's entrance. Children painted their own cubbies. Some of us (myself included) considered the cubbies both extremely ugly and unhygienic. It was not unusual to find lunch boxes and bags full of rotten food, sour milk, old science projects, hats and coats, along with many important keepsakes in the cubbies.

When the program expanded and Norma came on board, more cubbies were needed. Space was an issue. The structure gave way to shelves on which plastic dishpans are lined up. Each child makes a sign for the front of his cubby, and decorates it to suit himself. Coats and hats are now hung on hooks. Some of the hooks are in the hallway, others just inside the classroom door.

Scheduling

Scheduling of classroom activities changes constantly. The three teachers touch bases every morning before school starts, again at lunch, and several times in between. Still, things happen that are unexpected. Whole group activities, special visitors, plays, concerts, etc., are most often planned for the afternoons when they don't detract from Centers Time. Sometimes conflicts cannot be avoided. Parents who plan special activities only to have them cut short aren't always happy. Teachers have to exert themselves with some caution and make many judgments around scheduling matters.

The whole business of parent participation is a complicating factor in Charquin's scheduling. Babies get sick. Mothers get sick. Cars break down. Aunt Tillie comes to town unexpectedly. During flu season the parent volunteers who do show up may be stretched to the limit by the absence of sick participants. Since parents are volunteers, and not employees, the program can't make the same demands on them that an employer might. On the other hand, sometimes a parent gets a marvelous idea on his way to school, and this idea is not on anybody's schedule.

Charquin is loose by design. Long-range planning holds Charquin together. Regular weekly staff meetings are essential. All three teachers are involved. Often the meetings also include the field trip chairperson, the parent coordinator, and a spokesperson for one or more of the centers who may have a special need or may want to do a special project. At the meeting the successes and failures of the past week are discussed. Calendars are reviewed—both the weekly program calendar and the year-long calendar for field trips, fundraisers, resource persons, and special events. Calendar changes are noted in the newsletter and on the Parent Center bulletin board. They may also be placed on the Parent Group agenda.

Within the framework of the calendars, each teacher plans her own classroom schedule. They must keep in mind that an individual child may be with one teacher for one activity and another teacher for another activity and may also be doing a major project in a parent's center.

Coordinating with Markham School

Charquin is an alternative program and isn't obligated to attend to the bells except for opening, closing, and getting to the lunchroom on time— and even that's loose because Charquin students do not have to catch buses. At Charquin what's happening in the classroom takes precedence over externally dictated schedules. An effort is made not to interrupt children's learning activities because of the clock and the bells.

While learning experiences take priority over schedules, there are several reasons why it is important for Charquin to coordinate with and establish friendly relationships with the students and staff of Markham School. In the first place, the climate of the larger school has an impact on Charquin students and faculty who must share playground, lunchroom, library and other common spaces and resources. Furthermore, Charquin students eventually move out of Charquin and into the middle school with other Markham students. If this is to be a happy transition students must have friends outside of Charquin.

Therefore, whenever possible, Charquin plans its schedule to facilitate contact between Charquin students and other Markham students. Snack Time at Charquin is usually—but not always—about the same time as morning recess at Markham.

While Charquin attempts to coordinate its schedule with that of the larger school, scheduling is far more flexible, and routines which signal transitional times are unique. Bells which send students in other classrooms rushing for the door are ignored. Charquin children do not run for the door, neither do they have to line up or play the "I'm ready" game at recess and lunch time.

Dismissal routines are often a type of categorizing game which sometimes draws attention to little-known facts about the children. "If you're wearing red today you may go." "If you don't use hair spray..." "If you're a hog on mousse...." "If you didn't eat breakfast this morning..." Other times children are simply excused, "If you've finished and cleaned up, you may go."

Once released from Around the Rug, students proceed to their destination (lunch line, carpool, rest room or playground) via the back door, so that they don't bother other classes. Running, skipping, jumping rope, etc., enroute is perfectly acceptable. As a rule nobody watches them go. And, they usually arrive where they're going without incident.

When they are outside of Charquin, students know that they must answer to the authorities. This doesn't mean that Charquin's influence stops at the door. If parents don't like the way something is going on the playground or in the lunchroom, they discuss it in the Parent Group and plan a strategy. Personal strategies often prove the most effective—a parent who is noted for her diplomatic skill goes to the lunchroom or out to the playground with the children. She offers to help before she criticizes. Frequently the problem disappears just because she is there.

Not only are Charquin children trusted to walk themselves to the lunchroom, they may also chew gum and use the rest rooms as necessary. These practices say two things about Charquin's priorities. First, adults at Charquin don't feel the need to control kids. Kids are trusted and expected to control themselves. This isn't to say that children always behave appropriately. When they don't, the problems are discussed during Around the Rug, solutions are explored, and restrictions may be applied. Second, Charquin doesn't waste time teaching unimportant skills that the children will easily learn on their own, when needed. Children will never have to walk in line after leaving elementary school unless they participate in a marching band or go into the military. In both cases instructors will be available to teach the skill. Teaching "walking in line" in elementary school is a waste of teacher time. Charquin doesn't bother with it.

Scheduling to coordinate with Markham School requires special effort for teachers. Charquin may not attend to bells, but Charquin teachers still draw playground duty. If the class is finishing up a project, students may be left in the care of a couple of parents while the teacher goes out to the playground. Sometimes it takes special effort for a Charquin teacher—for whom recess is not a usual scheduling priority— to remember the duty schedule. The uniqueness of Charquin's program also raises issues around the scheduling of teacher prep periods.

Instructional Resources and Special Programs

As public school students, Charquin students are entitled to the same support services and special instruction that other school children receive. Several of them participate in the school's instrumental music program. Every year several Charquin children go to the speech therapist; several more see the reading specialist. Charquin's teachers are selective about making referrals of students to specialists. Parents play an active role in the decision-making.

Taking advantage of resource teachers and special services presents some issues. There is a problem of philosophy. Parents put their children in Charquin because they like what the program does. The child who goes to the resource room gets a very specific skills-based treatment. If immediate improvement is seen, parents don't object. But if it isn't, parents get worried about how much of Charquin the child is missing.

There are also logistical concerns. Charquin is such a busy place that it is easy for a young child to forget to go to the resource room. It takes cooperation between the child, the teacher, and the resource teacher, and sometimes the assistance of a parent to encourage the regular attendance that these services require.

Out-reach

There has at times been friction between the Charquin Program and the Markham School faculty, staff, and parents. Hayward schools have gone through years of budget cuts. The school is crowded. At such times programs that are different can become targets. On occasion the Charquin Parent Group has turned inward and become so concerned with the work of running the program that parents have not related to the needs of the larger school.

Today's Charquin members know that the environment of Markham School has an impact on Charquin and that working together with other parents and teachers is important. Charquin parents participate in PTA and fund-raisers. Charquin has brought assemblies and resource persons to the school. Parents and teachers have offered Family Math, Family Science, and other workshops to Markham's teachers and parents. These efforts, along with a fair bit of common courtesy, have resulted in generally good relations between Charquin and the rest of the Markham faculty and staff.

Summary

At Charquin the philosophy drives the classroom organization and the implementation of scheduling both internally and externally. Charquin's classroom environment is intentional. It is a constantly changing experiment which at times presents an untidy appearance, and can have both negative and positive outcomes. The individual desks that dominate the interior of the traditional classroom would be inappropriate for Charquin because the program's philosophy requires that students make many decisions, have a wide variety of activities and materials available, participate in the learning centers and engage in cooperative learning activities. At Charquin scheduling changes constantly. It is complicated by parent participation and held together by long-range planning. Coordinating with the schedule of Markham School is difficult, but making some concessions to that schedule is necessary for maintaining the health of the program and protecting the interests of Charquin students.

The Parent Group—Nuts, Bolts, Power, and Policy

Building Charquin is a lot like building a family. Every family needs an agenda around which to structure its activities. In some families the agenda is baseball. In other families it's church, or Dad's job (Curran, 60). The agenda of the Charquin family is promoting the participation through which all members—teachers, parents, and children—grow, learn, and play an authentic and valued role.

When a new family joins Charquin they are introduced before the parent group. They say a little about themselves and their children, why they've joined, what their interests are, and so forth. If the family has any special needs, those needs are made known to the group. Sometimes a family needs a car pool, or needs to exchange baby-sitting, or has a child who is sick or allergic. At this first parent group meeting an experienced family is appointed to help the new family learn the program. Whatever their needs and concerns, the new family learns that the parent group is a place to go.

Inclusiveness is one issue with which the parent group must deal. Charquin is an alternative school. There is a waiting list. Not everyone who wants in is admitted. Parents usually commit themselves to participate when they join. But the nature of parent participation in today's world is unpredictable. Even parents who make the commitment may see their lives change. Mothers return to work. Marriages are dissolved. Fathers' work hours change, etc.

Charquin teachers play an active role in building an inclusive family when they accept and acknowledge the gifts and efforts of all parents and make them feel welcome in the program. Charquin teachers become attached to their students and won't tolerate suggestions that some may not belong—even if their parents can no longer participate. It has always been Charquin's policy that once a child enrolls in Charquin she is part of the family. At Charquin, while participation is expected, inclusiveness and caring takes precedence.

The Parent Group

All parent participants are members of the Charquin Parent Group, which is the policy-making body. Teachers also attend parent group meetings. The parent group chooses a member to facilitate meetings. At Charquin, policy-making is a cooperative, democratic endeavor between the teachers and the parent group. The group meets once a month, usually on a Friday evening. Fridays present fewer conflicts with work and social commitments than do other weekday nights. Meeting on Friday also means that parents, teachers, and kids don't have to be out late on a school night. Most parents regard meetings as a family enterprise and participate on a regular basis.

As the program develops and changes, policies and practices are discussed and debated in the parent group. It is not unusual to hear a parent ask, "Is this who we are?" It's a way of asking whether the policy is consistent with Charquin's philosophy. It's a hard question to answer. The philosophy is understood mainly in terms of tradition, and new traditions keep evolving.

There are some things that the group handles well. The group manages fund-raising, votes on field trips, decides on major purchases, deals with public relations, handles proposals and presentations to administrators and the School Board, works with teachers on scheduling, agrees on instructional themes, encourages the classroom participation of parents, and acts upon specific requests of teachers. The parent group is a forum for presentations from those who would advocate new directions. As Charquin has moved toward a Whole Language approach to literacy, cooperative learning, manipulative math, and Writers' Workshop methods have been introduced. Consensus-building and parent education are important functions of the parent group.

There are some things that the parent group doesn't do well. "Constructive criticism" directed at participants, teachers, or children is generally not welcome. It is important for participants to feel good about what they are doing. Still, people do get criticized. Karen Rogge—a long time participating parent—suggested that we should write this simple statement into the new handbook: "You will be criticized." At some point everyone who takes responsibility for anything (and that's most participants) gets criticized. As in most families, good manners require a measure of tolerance. There's sometimes the question of whether the tolerance doesn't go too far. Issues often hang around for a long time before some perceptive member gets annoyed, names what is happening and calls it to everyone's attention. Naming the problem sometimes sets the stage for conflict. A major task of the parent group is managing conflict productively so that people can grow from the experience.

Power and Participation

One consequence of Charquin's latest expansion was that some participants felt the need for a more complex management system. This desire for change sparked a parent group debate. During the debate one parent stated the case for a loose organization emphatically: "I don't want to see this become a well-oiled machine....There's nothing wrong with letting new members learn some things the hard way." The debate went on for several years.

For parents the matter of organizational structure is really an issue of personal power. When things are too organized some people feel boxed-in—the need to ask permission dampens their creativity and limits their participation. The flip side is that for the less assertive parent, or the one who doesn't participate in the classroom regularly, rules are enabling. A clearly defined committee structure encourages such parents to participate at a higher level than they might otherwise. Power is a complicated matter at Charquin. If parents with different needs and different styles are to participate effectively there must be a balance that meets everyone's needs. That balance is hard to come by.

Power is also an issue for teachers. In order to teach, they need to have freedom, and the power to exercise their professional judgement without the interference of parents. Conflicts between parents and teachers can upset everyone and interfere with the instructional program. At Charquin power-sharing is a fluid arrangement which adjusts frequently to the situations and personalities of the moment.

Efficiency

On the matter of efficiency, a disclaimer seems in order. Here it is. Efficiency has never been Charquin's hallmark. Participation is what makes Charquin go. During parent group meetings participants say what is on their minds. If someone agrees with them, fine. If something needs to be done, volunteers are solicited. If someone agrees to do the job, it gets done—maybe. If not, it doesn't. Follow-up has always been a weakness. Charquin is labor intensive. It thrives on the willingness of parents and teachers to make personal contact with each other and with the children. Several program characteristics mitigate against efficiency. First, Charquinites tend to be people-oriented. They don't like bureaucracy. Second, reaching a consensus on what needs to be done is sometimes a long struggle. Often a job doesn't get done because the merits of doing it are still in doubt. Finally, there is the problem of figuring out who should do it. At Charquin this often means waiting for somebody to volunteer. The old army system is frowned upon. The assumption is that the person who really wants the job done will take responsibility for organizing the project and finding people to help out.

Committees, Communicating, and Coordinating

Resistance to bureaucracy not withstanding, Charquin's routines for communicating and accomplishing the task of running the program have become more organized in recent years. A handbook has been written and a more complex committee structure has emerged.

The *Charquin Parent Newsletter* has evolved from a single sided, hand-written sheet into a sophisticated computerized document. The newsletter provides parents, students, and staff with official information such as the minutes of parent group meetings, themes for the month, field trip schedules, fund-raising information and reports on activities in particular centers. There's also news about members and their families, advertisements of services and a wide variety of other information. The newsletter is an important instrument for sharing ideas, concerns and letters to the editor. It's published monthly and placed in parents' boxes in the Parent Center.

Other devices for communicating include the phone tree, the bulletin board and message center in the Parent Center, and daily journals in some of the learning centers. The phone tree is only used in emergencies. In these days of answering machines it's less speedy and reliable than it used to be. The message center and bulletin board are useful for reaching parents on their participation days. In some Charquin learning centers projects are on-going and a different parent is in charge of the activities each day. In such cases the daily journal of activities in the center is important for providing continuity of instruction. Parents make notes about what has been accomplished, what worked and what didn't. They may also make notes about the responses and work of individual children. When a parent arrives in the center in the morning they read the comments in the journal before they start their day's work. Before they leave the center at the end of the day they write their comments for the next day's parent.

Most of the work of running Charquin is accomplished through committees. Some subcommittees of the parent group are on-going. They are charged with such everyday tasks as field trips, clean-up, newsletter, publicity, networking, and fund-raising. Other subcommittees are charged with special short-term tasks such as developing the new philosophy, writing the handbook, or writing a proposal to be presented to the school board. Such a subcommittee dissolves when its task is complete. A subcommittee may involve as few as two or three members or as many as a dozen, depending on the job to be done and how many people want to be involved.

Curriculum committees coordinate the activities of parents within the various centers, in general terms, leaving specific daily lesson planning to individual parents. All parents who work in a particular center serve on the curriculum committee for that center. There are curriculum committees for cooking, art, gardening, and math, among others.

Teachers meet with curriculum committees on a variable schedule, depending on what the task of the committee is and how much guidance the parents seem to need. Teachers sometimes provide workshops for curriculum committees.

The Steering Committee is a recent addition to Charquin's committee structure. It came into being after the last program expansion. The Steering Committee coordinates the activities of the various committees and plans the agenda for parent group meetings. Each subcommittee and curriculum committee appoints one member to attend the weekly Steering Committee meeting. Teachers also attend this meeting. New ideas are tried out on the Steering Committee before they are presented to the parent group. Decisions of the Steering Committee are not binding. They can be appealed to the parent group. At Charquin all committees are responsible to the parent group.

Parent-teacher-liaisons, or "PTL," came into being after the last program expansion. The task of the PTL is to help parents address concerns without always taking them to a teacher. Protecting the teachers' instructional time and keeping teachers out of conflicts between parents is crucial if the classroom atmosphere is to be one that is conducive to learning. Of course, parents forget, and teachers spend much time troubleshooting. Still, if a problem comes to a teacher that he or she can't deal with adequately on the spot, there's someone to whom the parent can be directed. The purpose of PTL is to defuse issues before they loom large. Individual parents take their questions and problems to one of the parent-teacher-liaisons. These concerns may involve a teacher, a child, another parent, a policy, or just something that happened. The liaison asks whether this is a confidential matter and what the parent would like to see done about it. With the permission of the parent involved, one of several actions may be taken. The liaison may share information with the liaison from another classroom. The matter may be taken to the teachers. The liaisons may schedule a meeting to which all interested parents are invited (without teachers). Or, they may take the issue to the parent group. Confidential matters are never shared. The recommendations of PTL are not binding, unless they are addressed and voted upon by the parent group.

Modes of Participation

In some co-ops the pressure for parents to participate is coercive. In one alternative school of which I am aware, one parent's volunteer time is used up by keeping track of whether all other parents have done their time. In these situations the job of the parent group has been defined in terms of making sure that everybody does his or her part. In the end such systems often result in most parents simply putting in their hours, while others drop out and yet others are kicked out. Coercion engenders negative attitudes and discourages creative thinking and participation.

Charquin's parent group has kept the rules flexible. Over the years, parents who can't participate regularly have been encouraged to find alternative ways that they can help. Some of the long-standing tasks that such parents do include: cleaning the room in the evening, weeding the garden on week-ends, organizing fund-raisers, preparing materials, typing or word-processing newsletters, checking papers, and even doing extra carpool duty. Their contributions came to be called "alternative service," a title that some parents resent, but which still appears in the handbook.

At Charquin the task of the parent group is defined in terms of helping parents and giving them a positive sense that they belong to and are empowered by the group. In other words, the task of the group is not only to govern, but to help parents meet their needs and to support their self-esteem.

Support comes in many forms. Since Charquin sees itself as a family, it has always been considered appropriate to allow babies, both in the classroom and on field trips. It's understood that parents are responsible for the supervision of babies, and that they are also expected to participate. Most mothers of active toddlers will find another Charquin parent with whom they can trade baby-sitting on participation days. Still, babies in backpacks and preschoolers in the playhouse are common sights. Some children are Charquinites almost before they are born.

When people ask, "How does Charquin get so much parent partici-pation?" the only answer I can come up with is "attitude." Charquin's a good place to be. Program needs are clearly spelled out to parents. Their participation is both expected and appreciated. They are provided with educational opportunities. They are taken "seriously." And, they are allowed many options and much latitude for developing their job descrip-tions and fulfilling their commitment to participate.

Parents respond by coming through. As Linda Cano said, "One of my motivations for participating at Charquin, besides my concerns that my children get a good education, has been the fact that as hard as I work at Charquin, there are parents with me working just as hard if not harder. I'm inspired by the company of people I'm with. I have an Elementary School Teaching Credential, and some of my best mentors have been Charquin parents."

Teachers as "The Management"

Charquin's teachers have a unique and highly demanding position, one which requires both the confidence to try new things and the ability to bring others along. Charquin teachers not only work with children of many different ages in the same classroom, they manage and direct a wide range of parent participants. Notices that go home with children from Charquin are often signed "The Management." This term reflects a unique role, one unfamiliar to many teachers.

Charquin teachers do not view themselves as assembly line workers. They don't follow orders. They have management responsibility for a complex organization. This responsibility includes participating in the parent group, in much the same role as that of the director of a corporation or foundation. They are the professional resource people for all who participate in the program. Their success as teachers rests heavily on their ability to affirm, educate, and enable the many parents and children with whom they work.

As all of Charquin's teachers are keenly aware, parents are political creatures. When they join an organization they try to make themselves comfortable, get to know others, and learn the ropes. Soon they notice the points of tension and start trying to make changes. In so doing they often try to enlist the help of other members, and at times incur the wrath of established members and teachers who don't want to change.

Bob says that in the early years the political issues of parent participation really ate at him. Norma, Karen, and Dave have had their battles too. It would be more comfortable for teachers if parents would just come in and work and forget trying to influence the program and the conduct of others. But they won't. Teachers sometimes get irritated with the more political parents. If everyone gets worked up because someone didn't like the way a decision was made (or the way resources or time were allocated in a particular case) it's hard to give children the attention they need.

Later Bob became more philosophical about politics. He recognized it as part of the learning, growing process, and central to the kind of parent empowerment that is essential to maintaining a healthy program. He tried to use the issues that surfaced as opportunities for growth, and for bringing new information to bear on the debates.

When parents disagree, there are a number of underlying issues. Tenure is an issue. Parents who have been in the program longer just naturally assume that their ideas should have more weight. Workers vs critics is another issue. Parents who spend the most time in the classroom often assume that things should go their way. It's a kind of sweat equity. "I'm just here for the kids" is the battle cry. Teachers must be aware of the issues, and take care not to take sides.

The struggles that occur are opportunities to learn. Bob credits the challenge of working with parents for much of his professional growth. A few years ago when Bob took his masters' degree from the University of California at Berkeley, he said that it was the parents' demands for good information that forced him to enroll. Bob went on to participate in the

Bay Area Math Project, Bay Area Writing Project, and Equals. Later on he frequently presented in-service programs in math and language for parents and teachers throughout the Bay Area.

Bob kept a file of articles that addressed issues of learning theory and methodology. He learned to be firm in stating his limits and protecting his professional position. But Bob did sometimes compromise. At Charquin learning to deal with politics effectively is a major issue in teacher growth and development.

Charquin teachers shape the parent education component of the program. In this role they are major initiators of program change. When a teacher spends his summer reading, taking classes and workshops, and meeting new experts he often comes back to the parent group with ideas for projects and programs. He presents his ideas to the group, explaining exactly what it is that he wants to do, why, and what type of help he will need. He enlists the help of parents.

If he is promoting changes of major consequence—as Bob was when M&Ms, Menu, and Writers' Workshop were introduced—a teacher might encourage several likely parents to take special training. These parents then become a teaching team to help other parents. Sometimes they'll even offer workshops such as "Family Math," "Family Science," and "Writers' Workshop" to Markham School teachers and parents.

While this attention to guidance, training, and planning by teachers gives the program continuity and cohesiveness, some parents will never do it the teacher's way. Teachers must respect diversity, or risk pulling the program apart. It's a little like the Biblical parable of the wheat and the tares. The weeds can't be removed without destroying the crop.

Charquin teachers have a special relationship with parents. They spend many after school hours meeting with curriculum committees. In addition, they most often eat lunch with parents. While eating lunch with parents might seem like a little thing, it's quite unusual. Most public school teachers run to the teachers' room and eat lunch with colleagues, fleeing the isolation and stress of a classroom full of children which lacks adult companionship.

It's o.k. for a Charquin teacher to go to the teachers' room (and sometimes personally, or politically beneficial). But most days parents and teachers, babies and toddlers spend their lunch period sitting around the classroom at low tables, on floor cushions, or on the patio by the garden. They socialize, check papers, and prepare for the afternoon—while eating their sandwiches, tacos, and school lunch cuisine. (School age children usually go to the lunchroom, although small groups of friends will occasionally make special arrangements for a picnic on the patio.) This habit of eating lunch while working together probably got started because there is just so much work to do in Charquin. But, it seems as if participants gain strength from this daily ritual. They really enjoy the socializing. Teachers are valued members of the Charquin family. Family members take care of each other, even dispensing back rubs when needed.

Tradition and Development

In the original manuscript version of this book, the developmental history and tradition of what Charquinites call "The Charquin Family" was discussed in the first chapter. When I started passing the manuscript from one interested party to another, several persons asked why the history of Charquin is important. Wouldn't it be enough to describe the program as it is today?

At its heart the Charquin story is a story about process. The process that the program went through and the issues that participants encountered reveal something of what Whole Language people are facing as they seek to work from within the system to gain greater empowerment for all parents, teachers, and children.

Charquinites often refer to the program as a "family." It was a more apt term when the program was small. Today, with ninety children and all of their parents in the family, Charquin is more like a tribe. But the tag still sticks. The Charquin Family has history, icons, a distinct perspective and inside jokes. It initiates new members and changes and grows with them. The Charquin Family includes parents, grandparents, children, adolescents, teachers, younger siblings, and even the principal. Some of its members are with us, and others have gone before.

Sometimes Charquin adopts a member. Ann Cygielman took a group of children walking one day, looking for signs of spring. They found a "magical garden." When the owner drove up they visited with her, and were invited in for a look.

Mrs. Smith told them that she had built the garden herself. She was recovering from a back problem and could not take care of her garden as well as she would like. The children and Anne volunteered to help. A fast friendship developed. Mrs. Smith was invited to several school functions. Some of the children called her "grandma."

From the children's standpoint this family relationship means something special. At Charquin there's always a lap to sit on. Sometimes they sit on a parent's lap, and sometimes on that of an older child. When Around the Rug gets a little long and boring, five and six year olds often take advantage of the support. Parents are sometimes seen rocking an upset child in Norma's rocking chair.

Parents at Charquin often point out that children learn from one another, that this learning takes place in all kinds of settings, and that it is facilitated by the family environment. At other schools big boys don't play with little kids. At Charquin older boys not only play with little kids, they may also teach them. Some of their teaching is practical—I once watched Thomas show a group of younger children how to focus sunlight through a lens on dry twigs so that the twigs ignite. Other teaching is social. When Charquin children go out to play, finding ways to include the little ones is a consideration. Older children often change the rules for the benefit of the little ones.

The Charquin Family is an important support system for parents. Today's Charquin parents live in a culture where nuclear families are becoming increasingly isolated. Parents often work with colleagues who live at a distance and with whom they share few common interests. Grandparents seldom live nearby. At Charquin parents find other parents—people who share similar problems, joys, and frustrations. When these parents come together they talk. Since children are in mixed-age groups, the parent of a young child can talk to the parent of a child who is a couple of years older. The perspective of older parents—parents who aren't as far removed from the situation as say, a grandmother, is an important benefit for parents.

Sometimes all of the visiting in the classroom irritates teachers. When a room full of kids are working on cooperative projects while four or five parents are visiting in the corner, teachers remind parents that they're present to help kids. But parents point out that the kids don't need them all the time. They move out to the hallway and keep visiting about everything under the sun. Friendships started in the classroom carry over into the larger community as parents collaborate on projects and children

go home with their friends. Parents are brought together on the telephone, in the classroom, in car pools, and on field trips.

Charquin has a structure and process for dealing with issues and leaders who know the mine fields well. As with any family there are some issues that never go away, that must be struggled with anew periodically.

The Family Myths

As Sam Keen said in *Your Mythic Journey,* "Every family...has an elaborate system of stories and rituals that differentiate it from other families." Charquin's unique stories and myths and the celebrations through which these myths are remembered, relived, and revised, are central to the Charquin experience. The importance of tradition as a factor in Charquin's success should not be under-estimated.

Often visitors ask, "How can Charquin get parents (or the district administration) to agree to that?"

Frequently the answer is, "It's always been done that way."

Charquin's tradition carries with it a certain inertia. If somebody wants to change something that has always worked—or even something that hasn't worked—they need to convince a large number of people that a change will improve things. Even if the membership agrees, there's often foot-dragging. Furthermore, volunteers must be found to organize the project and take care of the matter.

To say that myths and traditions are central to Charquin is not to say that Charquin is tradition bound—it's not. Nor is it to say that the past was a Garden of Eden—it wasn't. Charquin is so dynamic that the past is easily either forgotten or idealized. Indeed, remembering requires a positive effort—and memory is often a trickster.

When a new policy is being debated and some questioning member asks, "Is this really what Charquin is about?" the group is challenged to come to a consensus about how they view history and how Charquin's history applies to the moment. Even if the group agrees on what the history is, the question arises as to which aspects of the Charquin tradition should be revered, and which should be overcome.

History sometimes gets lost or confused. The program's original by-laws were turned over to the district and have not been seen again. A number of years ago, when old members graduated, someone forgot to pass on the story of Charquin's escape from the Mission. There were various far-fetched stories about what made him noteworthy, and tradition had it that Charquin was an Ohlone Indian. (In fact, his tribal affiliation is uncertain.). It took a little digging through history books to find Charquin's story in *Native Americans of Northern California.*

Early Struggles

Charquin's traditions are rooted in a history of struggle. The first test was getting the district to agree to the proposal that established the program. Soon members found that being different often put the program in conflict with district leadership.

Several years after its establishment the district prohibited Charquin from advertising and forced out-of-district transfer students to withdraw. (Attendance officers actually entered the room and forcibly removed one young girl whose parents had not transferred her back to her home district.) Enrollment dropped to twenty-two students—and the district threatened to cut the program. Vigorous lobbying of the school board by parents saved Charquin. But there were hard days ahead.

The district, noting that Charquin had vacancies, transferred in several troubled students from other classes—students who weren't getting along where they were, and whose parents didn't buy into the parent participation format.

It was situations such as this that lead to the demise of most of the alternative public schools of the 1970s. Developing consensus on policy matters within a diverse group of parents was challenging at best. When the task was complicated by hostile policy from the administration of the school district, program survival was rare.

Charquin survived for a variety of reasons, including plain old fashioned luck. It is a tribute to the early members that despite the volatility of the situation, they were willing to continue working to develop a philosophy and a structure with which everyone could live.

Stories That Are Told

The documented history of Charquin is only part of the Charquin story. As is usually the case, there are a couple of versions of Charquin's history. One version is told by people who left the program and another by those who stuck in there. Furthermore, from one person to another there's considerable variation within the two versions.

When people who decided to leave Charquin tell their stories, they dwell on Charquin's early organizational problems. As their version goes, the founders of Charquin were good at making the political points and getting the program started, but weak on implementation in the classroom.

To make matters worse, the group tended to argue among themselves. Those who left say that the loose management style was a problem for them.

Bob, as well as other long-time Charquinites, confirm that the criticism of people who left Charquin are not without merit. Charquin was a product of the idealism of the 1970s. Direct democracy, participation, and individualism were core values. Many of Charquin's founders had unpleasant memories of authoritarian schools. They wanted something different for their children. Freedom was a big concern. Spontaneity and a hang loose attitude characterized program management. Field trips were frequent and often involved little planning. If everyone wanted to go this morning, the group went. For some people this degree of spontaneity was undesirable. Consequently, the group had difficulty in agreeing on what activities should be required of students, parents, and teachers. Early newsletters reveal that people often bickered and looked out for their own interests.

Then there's the other story. Those alumni who stuck it out through the rough times tell of their commitment to the Charquin community. It's not that they weren't concerned about academics—many of them were. But the community, the friends they made, and the social context of school was important to them.

These alumni reflect on Charquin's warmth and caring. They tell about a program that helped children deal with the social and emotional realities of their lives. They remember the friendships that developed, the shy children who learned self-esteem, how to talk before the group, feel powerful, and make decisions. These Alumni reminisce about the good times they had and laugh about the hard times. They tell how participating in the program promoted their self-esteem and empowerment, and resulted in lasting friendships.

Bob's Role

During the 1970s the life expectancy of an alternative school in the public system was eighteen months (Deal, 15). Many of these schools depended on the leadership of a charismatic individual (Bakalis, 224). For Charquin, Bob was the leader. Bob was good-humored. He helped everyone hang loose. He was able to work with people calmly, hear their concerns, and defuse problems and criticisms before they got out of hand. He was committed. He learned and grew with the parents and students. Charquin beat the odds.

One of the reasons that Charquin lasted is that Bob distanced himself from the public political scene—limiting himself to lobbying administrators behind the scenes for the things that the program needed. When a vote of the School Board was needed on an issue, parents wrote, presented, and defended the proposals. Bob was usually in the board room to listen. While parents were preparing presentations, Bob kept his ears open and fed them information about what was being said by whom, and what concerns needed to be addressed. In public he did not put himself forward as the leader.

Bob and the Parent Group discouraged any unnecessary political activity on behalf of Charquin. Parents were encouraged to be involved, informed, and active in PTA and on district committees. But saying anything on behalf of Charquin in public—especially if it sounded like a complaint—was definitely discouraged, unless the Parent Group had agreed on what was to be said.

Parents and Teachers Learning Together

At Charquin learning and growing has always been the most important activity. As the program developed, so did its participants. The skillful leadership of teachers, and the adherence of the group to its democratic tradition facilitated learning and program development.

Bob had to learn how to be an Open Classroom teacher on his own. The district was pushing in the opposite direction. Early newsletters report Bob's frustration with district demands for paperwork, particularly with regard to the reading program. The principal evaluated the program in 1977. She emphasized the goods results on standardized tests and how the program had improved since schedules and routines had become regularized—in other words, less open. The evaluations noted that children were now using district approved texts in reading, math, spelling, and language. Furthermore, the schedule resembled "academic periods." The school principal viewed the new structure as a "welcome change in a positive direction."

To be sure, in the early days some of the things Bob did were not open. Bob joked about himself as the "benevolent dictator." He placed students in reading, language, and math groups more-or-less by ability. During the morning hours children went from center to center to meet with their various groups while Bob taught reading. In the afternoons Bob taught social studies. Parents taught art and science and finished projects begun in the morning.

In these early years Bob needed control. Parents who were tired of disorganization and conflict gave him latitude. Neither Bob nor the parents were satisfied with the new regime. Oddly enough, it may have been these early concessions to the values of the system that eased the fears of administrators so that they looked the other way as Bob and the parents learned, grew, and decided to set out on a more open approach.

By 1979, as the children and parents became more competent and dependable and Bob gained experience as a teacher, his need for structure and control declined. He agreed to allow the children to move from center to center individually, rather than in groups. The academic periods were eliminated so that children could leave a center and move on when they were done. Ability grouping effectively disappeared in all centers except reading. As previously noted, the approach to reading also became more holistic.

While Bob organized, and even dictated, he remained sensitive to the feelings of parents, and convinced of their value as educators. Bob became the leader and the role model. He paid close attention to building an environment and personal relationships within the program that encouraged parents to accept more responsibility and try new things.

Bob was not too quick to solve problems that belonged to parents. When parents didn't show up to participate he let the kids know that "I guess we won't be having science, (or art, etc.) this morning because ... isn't here." Kids went home and leaned on their parents. When the room became dirty and disorganized, Bob would send out a notice informing the membership that help was needed. Things fell into a rhythm. From year to year parents could predict the timing of such events as Bob's yearly letter which went something like: "Everybody's had the flu. We're missing a lot of you on your participation days... (Pep talk and guilt trip)... Let's get with it. You're needed."

While Bob expected a lot of support from parents, he steered away from criticizing them. As Bob puts it, "They have to want to be here. It must ultimately be an enjoyable place and experience." Safety and humor became the hallmarks of Charquin. Because parents felt safe, they took chances, tried new things, and learned. Their expertise as teachers developed. Their contributions to the program increased. They learned to support each others' efforts and work together to meet group objectives.

As the Charquin Program matured, Charquin parents developed their teaching skills and became active partners in program development. Often parents who were excited about a new method would go outside the program for more training and then become trainers themselves. Bernie Homen, Karen Rogge, JoEllen Rice, Susan Rockwell, Christina Sylvester, among others, have taken Family Math, Math Their Way, Math Solutions, Family Science, and Writers' Workshop courses so that they could help develop process-oriented writing, math, and science programs at Charquin. After taking these workshops these parents not only worked with the children, they also presented workshops for Markham parents and teachers.

Bernie, Christine, and Karen told me that they had chosen to work in math because they had experienced a discouraging math program during their own school days and wanted Charquin children to have something better. Their participation taught them a great deal about math and a lot about how children learn.

Other Charquin parents have learned a lot, too. A couple of parents have gone on to become public school teachers and several more are considering the possibility. After years of managing Charquin's cooking center, Kent Faulk started teaching Cajun cooking in the adult school. Leslie Faulk enrolled in the horticulture program at Chabot College. Roxanne, Gargi, and Gloria Holleman also developed interests at Charquin and went on to teach their specialities at the adult school and in park and recreation district classes. Roxanne is now the children's art specialist at The Sun Gallery.

Charquin parents develop skills of all kinds. Several parents have met success in writing grant applications. Some have developed computer literacy. As parents work with children and discover that they have something to share, their self-esteem and teaching skill develop. They learn how to ask questions, facilitate exploration, and listen for answers instead of giving answers. As parents learn that they don't have to have all of the answers, their confidence in themselves and the children grows. They become able to move away from structured curriculum models.

One example of how teaching style evolves as parents grow happened in the Art Center. A few years ago parents in the Art Center used district curriculum guides to structure the art program. One unit might emphasize line. Another time color would be discussed and special projects would be planned using color as a theme. But the parents got bored with this approach. They started watching and involving themselves in what the children were doing. As time went by parents gave less attention to planning sequential skills-based lessons. They developed long-term projects in drawing, painting, jewelry-making and pottery that went on for weeks on end. The children came up with their own ideas and were anxious to get to the Art Center every morning to work on their projects. Art Center parents discovered that children really learn all of the basics of art if a good art teacher watches them, talks with them, listens to their problems, uses correct vocabulary in describing the situations that are encountered, shows them things, and helps them make new discoveries. In other words, the teaching of art is a holistic experience—it is guided by the spirit within, a spirit which responds more to ideas, questions, and experience than to directions, carefully structured plans or the acquisition of a segmented sequence of skills.

As parents learn and grow, their confidence in themselves and in the children increases. As confidence increases, their need for structuring activities and for placing performance requirements on students declines. They start looking at the products the children produce and the concepts they are mastering, rather than the blanks they are filling in. It's the same process that new teachers go through.

This developmental process in learning to teach means that experienced parents and teachers must encourage, support, and be patient with each other and with new parents. It means that the program has never really arrived, in the sense that everyone is employing Whole Language philosophy and methods. The program is always building and recycling. It's the same process that sometimes gives the classroom the appearance of disorder. Just as people never quit learning and trying new things, the environment is never really finished and put away either.

Traditional Roles and Activities

As with any family, there are traditional roles and activities that serve important functions in organizing group life. Parent participation and "Pow Wow," (now called Around the Rug) are traditions that date back to the founding days. In the beginning Pow Wow was much as it is today, except that parents who were concerned about peace issues, or involved in drug abuse prevention programs and other such endeavors were more likely to share their political concerns and activities with children. It was not unusual for Charquin students to participate in marches and walk-a-thons for one cause or another.

Parent participation in the classroom, in policy making, and in program management is the tradition that most clearly sets Charquin apart from standard practice. Charquin parents take heavy responsibility for planning and implementing the program. Parents aren't just helpers, they're full partners in the program. They fulfill an amazing array of program needs, from carpooling and participating in meetings to teaching, preparing materials for classroom use, cleaning, work parties in the garden, supervising outdoor activities, organizing field trips, word processing, copying, writing, editing, and presenting workshops.

Just for the record, Charquin parents are teachers. This doesn't mean that they confuse their role with that of the professional teachers who are in the classroom every day. Bob, Norma, and Karen have the final word on day-to-day matters, and on any issue that the Parent Group has not decided. They are the professionals, and parents must accept their guidance.

The students also know the difference between the teachers and the parents. They use the words, "My teacher says..." in much the same way that other children do. If a child is trying to make a point he may appeal to the authority of a parent who works in one of the centers and is an expert in a certain field. More than once I've found myself checking with Sherry or Judy on matters of scientific fact and asking Terry whether snakes really do what my child claims that "Terry says" they do.

The role of parents is not one that was prescribed in documents or dictated by a certain format. Parents developed their role through a long process of growing, learning, and working together. It didn't come easily. There were—and still are—many fights along the way. The role of parents is not a static one. Parents continue to carve out new and unique niches for themselves. Every summer brings the question: "What's going to be different this year?"

Icons and Inside Humor

As with any community rooted in history, Charquin has icons and a certain brand of inside humor. The Doy Face logo is Charquin's favorite icon. The Doy face is a caricature of a hapless individual with buck teeth, sagging eyes, a big nose, and frazzled hair. His big tongue hangs out the side of his mouth, he's drooling, and a fly is buzzing around his head. Children learn early to draw the Doy Face. It adorns Tee-shirts, aprons, and many of the children's papers and notes. The Doy Face is Bob's creation. He's a gifted cartoonist who values humor and inflicts it daily on parents and children.

The word *Doy* has many different meanings, something like *Uff Da'* in Norwegian. It can mean clumsy, disorganized, almost funny, late, I don't know what to say, etc. *Doy* is usually said with emphasis and a certain expression, with the mouth slightly askew and the tongue hanging out.

There's a lot of teasing at Charquin. A casual observer might think that some of this teasing borders on meanness. It really doesn't. Charquin teasing carries with it a certain caring attitude, a recognition that "we're all in this together, and nobody's perfect." Charquinites usually don't get hurt by a tease. In fact, they tend to like the attention.

Most Charquinites have at least one nickname. These nicknames range anywhere from a pun on the person's real name to something odd that only a Charquinite would understand. Names such as "Furnace," "Bushes," "Justino," "Justin two," "Python," and "The Italian Stallion," hold special meanings within The Charquin Family. Parents and teachers are not immune from nicknames either. There are "Roxy," "Dickie Poo," "Abby Normal," and "The Despot," among others. In Charquin having a nickname is honorific. Some kindergartners don't feel as if they've made it until they have one.

Charquin humor is both written and oral. Cartoons are important. Charquin kids are connoisseurs of cartoons. They clip their favorites and bring them to school, often saving them in notebooks or taping them to the door. Some Charquinites become good cartoonists. Bob does a lot of drawing and the kids model his activity.

No one, inside or outside of Charquin, is immune from humor. At Charquin politicians come in for a fair amount of kidding. A few years ago a student, Jared Mariconi brought in an old poster of Ronald Reagan at the O.K. Corral. The poster was hung in a place of honor, with a small flag taped to it. The flag kept getting moved around from one vital location to another.

Some of my favorite Charquin humor comes home as memos to parents. Such memos are handwritten, decorated with Doy faces and other cartoon images, and replete with phonetic spellings, and non-standard grammar. If someone wants to disseminate information to parents, he takes it to Bob for suitable art work. Word processed materials, like those sent out from the district office, just don't get the same reading that a Charquin memo does.

Celebrations and observances

As with all families, the Charquin family has traditional observances and celebrations. See-Ya-Bye is the biggest and best family celebration.

Alumni congregate. Kids prepare skits, musicals or plays. *Don't Fence Me In* is sung. The quilt that the children and Linda Cano worked on all year is raffled. Food is brought to the multi-purpose room. Everyone eats and makes merry and hugs each other good-bye for the summer. Parents know that it's not really good-bye. The phone rings early the next morning and weeks of running kids back and forth across town to their best buddies' houses begin. The garden needs to be watered over the summer and veggies need to be picked. There are birthday parties and casual get-togethers before school starts again.

The school year brings a Halloween trip to the pumpkin patch and the Fitzgerald Marine Reserve. This annual trip dates back many years. On Thanksgiving a turkey is barbecued on the patio. At Christmas time children draw names and make gifts at home for the child whose name they have drawn. Giant cookies, gingerbread houses, homemade candy, and all sorts of crafts are exchanged. The teachers' desks are always piled high with goodies. In the spring the whole group takes a family camping trip to Memorial Park.

Celebrating together builds a sense of community. Traditional rituals become deeply ingrained. The year after my child graduated we found ourselves driving past Markham on the way home from a doctor's appointment at 11 A.M. on the day before Thanksgiving. As we passed the school Justin said, "I bet everybody's getting ready to eat the turkey." I was thinking the same thing at that very moment!

Charquin's yearly observances include Kids Teach Parents Day. On this day children run all of the centers, and parents must do the lessons.

Doy Bucks Week is a yearly observance. During Doy Bucks week children get paid or charged for everything they do and use (pencils, paper, trips to the bathroom, not raising a hand before speaking, turning in assignments on time, going to centers, etc.) Bob designed the play money. Each denomination is a different color, and has a Doy face in the place where US money has the image of a president. At the end of the week there's an auction. With their Doy Bucks Children can buy comic books and other items that have been donated by parents and friends.

Students often come up with rather advanced accounting devices and savings strategies as part of Doy Bucks week. One year a group of fourth grade boys started a 'money club.' They amassed a fortune. One member of the club put the group's funds in a box with his mother's teaching materials and forgot where he put it. A fiscal emergency and much angry

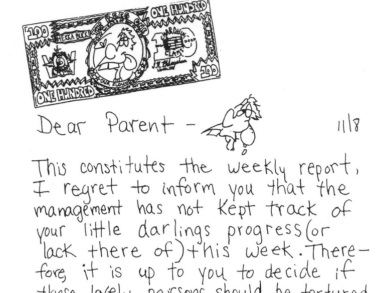

Dear Parent —   11|8

This constitutes the weekly report,
I regret to inform you that the
management has not kept track of
your little darlings progress (or
lack there of) this week. Therefore, it is up to you to decide if
these lovely persons should be tortured
as usual, or simply set loose on
the greater East Bay for a weekend of unbridled yuck-yuck.
The usual reports will continue next
week.
                    Yourz, D. Slob.

speculation about where the funds had gone rocked the classroom. It was finally decided that the classroom's money supply was not seriously out of balance, and that no individuals seemed to have more money than they could reasonably have been expected to obtain by honest means. The losers accepted their loss (not without grumbling) and the classroom returned to normal. The Doy Bucks were found the following year when the parent once again needed that particular box in order to repeat a center activity for Doy Bucks Week.

New Members

Charquin initiates new members into the program and gives them full membership rights—although most new members complain that they don't really feel like full members for a couple of years. These new members both change the program and are changed by it.

When early Charquinites return for a visit, they sometimes wonder whether today's parents have a clue as to what Charquin was really about back then. They probably don't. The emphasis on Native American culture is missing, except for the program's curiosity provoking name and occasional social studies units. The old Charquin lacked a high level of organization and the many committees that characterize today's program.

Today's young parents are removed from the life-styles of the hippie era. They want many of the same things: peace, love, joy, and a success-oriented program. But they aren't as opposed to placing performance requirements on children and structuring the children's time as means of promoting academic success.

As new parents enter Charquin they present the program with a challenge. Parents need to become full partners in the dialogue and empowered through the democratic process, even before they fully understand the meaning and workings of the program. Charquin has remained as open as it is largely because the debate proves educative to most new members.

A Family with Perspective

The Charquin Family has a distinct perspective. Basic to the Charquin tradition is a certain attitude toward children. At Charquin children are not to be ordered around, or yelled at. They are to be listened to, allowed to make decisions, respected, and cared for. Their feelings are important. When a child tells about an experience, he is frequently asked, "How did that feel?" Parents and children are expected to care about what they do and about how what they do impacts the lives of others.

This does not mean that things always go well. When a parent breaks the behavior code it is not the "teacher's job" to set him right. The teacher may have something to say about it. Ideally a parent who has observed the problem approaches the offender during a private moment with words of encouragement, wisdom, or a question about what is going on. This is a difficult role for parents, and it's not always well handled.

Sometimes there is gossip. At other times the issue is brought up in a parent group meeting and results in more embarrassment than anyone needs. As in any family, things aren't always smooth. Occasionally a parent who is embarrassed or has an honest disagreement will back off from program participation. On a number of occasions I have heard parents discussing how an estranged parent might be encouraged to become active again. It's a sticky matter. Sometimes a parent drops out. Usually they stay, work out their differences, grow and learn.

A central tenet of the Charquin perspective is that children should be free to select and participate in projects and activities of their own choosing. Charquin participants have always argued that empowering children nurtures their self-esteem. At times the matter of giving children freedom to choose comes into tension with other values—especially when a child is slow in learning to read or seems irresponsible. In these situations the question inevitably arises, "How should authority be imposed?" Parents and teachers spend much time debating which activities should be required, and which should not.

Charquin has an explicit political perspective. This perspective rests on the ethics and morality that the program practices. It's a position that says to members, "We're here to build a better world. We all have a responsibility to work together to do that."

In the early days Charquin students often participated in peace marches and fund raisers for social service organizations. They wrote letters to politicians about these and other matters. For a few years the program was relatively inactive politically. Recently political activism surfaced around the issues of building a new freeway through town and the Gulf War.

Some parents disapprove of political activism in the classroom. To others such resistance raises the question of whether Charquinites have forgotten who they are. It's a healthy source of tension in the program. Both sides are listened to. Decisions are made democratically, and sometimes participants are given the choice of whether they wish to participate in a given activity.

Some Issues Never Go Away

As my childhood piano teacher used to say, "Practice makes perfect." The kind of practice to which she was referring was a repeated effort to become proficient at rendering someone else's composition. The task at Charquin is not only to deliver, but to compose the program.

Charquin has developed, and is still developing, both its philosophy and its methodology. Some issues never quite get settled. Parents who worry about test scores, accountability, homework, discipline, and how their kids will get along in the middle school push in one direction. Parents who prize openness, ownership, and experientially-based learning pull in the other direction. Old-timers smile and nod. Every year the theme repeats with a new variation. Every year the answers are a little different. The gray area is always large. The positive value of difference is that it creates a social context for dynamic consensus building.

Assessment

Assessment is a central issue in any educational endeavor. The best-looking program is no good unless it can show that it does what it says it does. At Charquin there are two major issues in assessment. First is the assessment of student progress. Students, teachers, and the district office all need to know how students are doing. The second issue is monitoring the health of the program and the satisfaction of its members.

Assessment of Student Progress

At Charquin the purposes of assessing student progress are somewhat different than in traditional classrooms. Since a child stays with the same teacher for several years and all program teachers are familiar with his work and personality, there is no need to pass assessments on to another teacher at year's end—until the child is ready to leave the program. Charquin parents who teach in the program would find traditional report cards far too superficial to meet their needs. Their central concern in assessing student progress is making judgments about where the child is in his learning so that his educational experience can be planned appropriately.

Charquin's practices for assessing student progress date back to the Open Classroom model and have not changed very much. There are no grades and no conventional report cards. Teacher assessments of student progress are based largely on the quality of student work and on the concept development that students exhibited during group and personal interactions. Children keep journals, save their work in notebooks, display it on walls and in the hallway, present it orally before the class, and take it home frequently. Teachers read and comment on student journals and keep records of work completed.

The entire teaching team—parents as well as teachers—provides the information on which assessments of student progress are based. Everyone knows all of the children and informally share much information about students with each other. Parents assist with correcting papers and record keeping.

Sharing information with parents and involving them in the decisions relating to children is important because parents are teaching in the classroom—and teachers are more effective when they know more about their students. (Standardized test scores and information on psychological and remedial referrals are, of course, privileged information, available only from the teacher to the parent of the child involved.)

Teachers are not the parents' only source of information regarding the performance of their children. It is not unusual to hear a parent checking on a child's performance with another parent. Parents obtain much useful information from one another. The teachers likewise ask parents, "How did Johnny do in your center this morning?"

While parents and the entire teaching staff have access to a lot of information about individual children and they share their observations with teachers, it is the teacher to whom the child is assigned who has responsibility for taking this information, evaluating it, shaping it into recommendations for action, and sharing his judgments with parents and faculty.

Teachers schedule times for in-depth conversations with individual parents. Once or twice a year each parent has an individual conference with the teacher, at the teacher's request. Additional conferences may occur at the request of parents.

There are usually one or two children who express their emerging independence by refusing to be productive. Bob regularly scheduled weekly conferences with the parents of a couple of these students. Topics discussed sometimes included assignments due, compliance with deadlines, projects undertaken, progress with social problems, and academic progress. If a student was having learning problems the teacher would check to see whether parents had followed through with promises to help—and how it was going. New approaches and materials might be suggested.

These meetings often began with the parent walking in on Friday afternoon and asking Bob, "Well, what does Sally have to do this evening before she can go to the beach (or somebody's birthday party) this weekend?"

Bob would call in the student, and give a quick run-down. Parent, student, and teacher would spend a couple of minutes reflecting on whether things were getting better or worse, why, and what other approach might do the job. Parents and teachers didn't gang up on the kid. They sought her cooperation, and her in-put—without accepting flimsy excuses.

Charquin teachers call parents any time they think that assistance, coordination, or follow-up between home and school will be helpful. The focus of parent-teacher contacts is to promote student performance and parent participation in the educational process.

Although keeping parents informed about how their children are doing is important, it is the student whose job it is to learn. She has the greatest need to know.

At Charquin Doy faces, "Wow great!," "Yeah!" "Right on!" "Try again," and "See Me," in brightly colored felt pen replaced the usual grades of "A,B,C...." When reading journals Bob took pains to make comments that connected his life story with that of the student. "Yeah, that happened to me once. It worked out different." He often wrote questions in the margins. "How did that feel?" "'Do you think that was the right thing to do?" "Why?"

When students work in small groups parents have the opportunity to share their experience, ask questions, and provide immediate feed-back. Immediate feed-back is important. Students who must wait until 3 P.M. on Friday to find out how they did on an assignment (as is often the practice in traditional classrooms) frequently lose interest in the project before their questions are answered.

Probably the most effective means of assessment of student productivity comes from the group rather than from the marking of papers. Charquin students spend a great deal of time sitting around the rug listening to each other share their reports, stories, and solutions to math problems. They learn to listen, question, evaluate, and share their ideas about each others's work.

The student's ability to listen and question didn't happen automatically. Students had to learn how to critique each others' work. As every teacher knows, children are sometimes tempted to put their feelings about the report-giver into their critique of his work—being either mean or sugar-candy-superficial. Sometimes children don't pay close attention and end up with no questions. And other times they just play it safe and polite. Teachers set the tone and establish the rules. A mean critique isn't accepted. Probing questions are modeled. When students aren't attending, and aren't going beneath the surface, the problem is pointed out and discussed. When cooperative group assessment is working, it is far more effective than the correcting and grading of papers by the teacher. It provides students with more immediate feedback and a more diverse source of information. The process itself causes students to reflect upon what they have done and upon their thinking as they did it. This reflective activity turns assessment into a learning endeavor.

State and District Testing Programs

One thing hasn't changed over the years. To date the district administration has shown no interest in developing appropriate assessment measures that can validly display and discriminate among the various abilities and concepts that Charquin teaches. Program students take the same battery of tests that all other district students take. That battery now involves three different yearly tests, as compared to only one back in the early days. The district requires the *Comprehensive Test of Basic Skills* (CTBS). The state requires that the district give a district-designed minimum proficiency test, *Reach*, as well as the *California Assessment Program (CAP)* tests.

In general the tests have little diagnostic value. CTBS and CAP scores are reported long after the tests are administered—and in the case of CAP they give no individual results. The tests cost the district and the State a bundle. The amount of instructional time and program disruption required to test all of the students in a multi-age grouped classroom is an issue.

A major problem with all of the tests is that, just like the casual observer who doesn't understand a messy room, the tests focus on end products, neatness and skills. They are not designed to shed light on the process of learning, or the attitudes, behaviors and content that Charquin teaches.

Most of Charquin's older students do well on the required tests. The mismatch is most obvious for the younger students. On the *Reach* test older children have little difficulty. Several of them usually get the essay portion of their test displayed in the district office. Charquin's younger children often fail the test. While they typically write creative stories that are longer and use more words than do other children of their age, their invented spelling and penmanship count against them. (Their penmanship isn't always as neat as that of students who do daily penmanship drills).

The mismatch between Charquin's instructional objectives and the skills evaluated on standardized tests is also obvious on the CTBS test. Once again, older students do well and younger children have difficulty. At the first and second grade levels the CTBS is essentially a test of phonics. Since Charquin's Whole Language methods don't stress phonics, the younger children are often frustrated.

If the program and the district are to have a clear picture of exactly what Charquin students learn, more appropriate assessment procedures must be developed. For the time being, parents and teachers draw on their experience and look to the older children for proof that the little ones will eventually learn all that the tests evaluate—and more.

Challenges and Changes

Since the latest program expansion, the larger program and the presence of older children have drawn Charquin's traditional assessment routines into question. For older children assessment is a more complex issue. Parents of young children can readily observe the growth in literacy and sociability. They don't feel a need for a detailed reporting system. For older children the growth is not as easily observed by parents, particularly those who are not in the classroom frequently. In addition, more older children have parents who are unable to participate in the classroom regularly.

At the time of the last program expansion there was, for parents of older children, a great uncertainty about whether their children would be well prepared to move on to the intermediate school. Parents feared that since the intermediate school was part of the system, students coming from traditional classrooms would find the transition easier. The nervousness of parents showed up in demands for more homework and more discipline. They wanted regular feedback, including weekly reports of assignments completed.

Bob didn't like weekly reports. They skewed the program and emphasized doing assignments and homework rather than mastering concepts. Satisfying the parents' need for reassurance required more record keeping than teachers might ordinarily do. But the teachers bowed to parent demands, as long as parents helped out by correcting papers and keeping records. Weekly reports are no longer a practice. Parental nervousness subsided after the first couple of classes did well in intermediate school. The last program expansion presented another challenge to traditional routines. The larger number of students, parents, and teachers in the program complicates the matter of cooperation among teachers and parents in the assessment of students. Both Bob and David expressed concern over knowing the younger children—and their parents—less well than they used to. This is a serious concern, both because the younger children move up and because informal assessment practices work far better in situations where teachers, parents, and students know each other extremely well. When people know each other less well there are implications for what types of information need to be shared and for the means by which it is shared.

The larger program also made grouping for instruction a more complicated matter. Grouping decisions often depend on assessment decisions. While most grouping continues to be flexible and not according to ability, teacher assessments may influence the decision whether or not to move a child from one room to the next with the rest of the children of his age group. This raises the question of whether or not a child has learned what is expected, an issue in which parents have both a practical and an emotional stake.

Parents are involved in grouping decisions. Generally speaking, parents don't mind if their child is promoted ahead of other children her age. What they do mind is if she is left behind her age group. In such cases the parents must agree that the decision is in their child's best interest. All parents expect for their children to learn. They demand explanations if it appears that she isn't learning.

Concerns about grouping were partially addressed in 1990 when younger children were given an assessment from *Math Their Way*. It was given orally and individually. Older children were given a teacher-designed assessment at the same time. Assessments in other curriculum areas have not been so formalized. Decision-making about grouping remains a fairly subjective matter—one in which parents have a lot of input. Students are sometimes given choices.

The issues are not yet settled. The program for the older children has spent its first several years experimenting with different structures, much as the fledgling program for younger children did fifteen years ago. Whole Language experts recommend anecdotal systems for keeping track of children's developmental progress. (see Goodman, Bird, and Goodman, 1991, and Goodman, Goodman, and Hood, 1988). And even the U.S. Department of Labor recommends such a system. It's a promising field that's still developing.

After Charquin: Follow-up

No follow-up studies have been done on Charquin students. Instead, the program has relied on the fact that Charquin is a community where people tend to stay in touch with each other over time. It is an old tradition for students to return to the program for a visit after receiving their first report cards at the intermediate school. Bob always copied report cards and pinned them to the bulletin board behind his desk. They made an impressive display, and worked to calm the fears of children and parents who were about to move on.

Evaluating the Program

Charquin does a yearly program review. This review focuses on parent perceptions of the program, its livability and effectiveness. The review process takes a little different form each year. Traditionally it consists of a questionnaire. The questionnaire is developed by a committee of parents and teachers. Before constructing the questionnaire, this committee solicits information from the membership. They do this to insure that the most timely questions are asked.

Several different types of questions are asked. Parents are asked to give the ages of their children so that their responses can be reported by age-group. The questionnaire may include several multiple choice questions. Some questions may ask a parent to rate his satisfaction with some area of the program's performance. This rating may be done on a scale of one to ten, with a space for comments. There are usually two or three short essay questions. Each question focuses on one major program concern, such as teacher performance, parent performance, student achievement, curriculum, environment, instructional methods, or classroom routines.

Each family is asked to fill out one form, noting answers on which both parents may not agree and answers which may be different for their different children (if they have more than one child in the program). Ample time is allotted at the parent meeting so that all parents can fill out the questionnaire. Parents are told well ahead of time at which meeting this will happen. Questionnaires are placed in the Parent Center boxes of parents who missed the meeting, with an urgent request to return it immediately. (As in any such procedure, questionnaires that go home often do not come back). Participants are asked not to put their names on the questionnaire. Returned questionnaires are divided into stacks, depending on the ages of the respondents' children. Each question is reviewed separately. Responses to scale questions or multiple choice questions are tallied. For the short answer and essay questions, typical responses are noted. Atypical responses are listed.

Results are discussed with the teachers. A report is made to the Parent Group. The group is asked for feedback, both on the process and on the results of the review. Since product improvement is the point of the assessment exercise, the Parent Group must consider both the implications of its findings and the recommendations of parents and staff as to how the review might get better information. Once the program review has been presented to the Parent Group, the teachers and parents consider new directions for the coming year.

The Politics of Assessment

Several years ago Nancy Honig addressed a conference that I attended. I asked her why her husband, the California State Superintendent of Public Instruction, was so committed to his California Assessment Program. Nancy argued that the tests were politically necessary. She claimed that legislators and voters just won't vote for school funding measures unless they can see test results that show that the schools are working.

This strategy works unreliably, at best. The scores rise and fall by fractions of a point in successive years, or soar for no apparent reason. Voters and politicians don't understand what the scores mean, because they don't mean much. But school teachers spend months preparing students to take the tests.

Test scores have been a two-edged sword for Charquin. At one point (when Charquin served students only through the third grade) Charquin students developed a reputation for testing high and entering the Gifted and Talented Program upon leaving Charquin. Once in GATE they were assured top track classes through high school. This made the program attractive to ambitious parents who weren't always committed to holistic instructional practices. Since the program adopted Whole Language methods, older children generally test well, while the test scores of first and second graders are often not impressive. Parents who harbor academic ambitions for their children get nervous early on and create some pressure for a more academic emphasis—pressures that teachers and old-line traditional Charquin parents resist.

Charquin tries to ignore the tests and depend on good public relations and parent education to develop support for the program. When celebrations occur or awards are won, press releases are sent out to newspapers and television stations. Letters to the editor are written about important matters. Teachers and parents cultivate good relations with the local press and politicians and stay in touch with a long list of alumni. Politicians, civic leaders, and citizens are often invited into the classrooms for special occasions. Many of them come.

Charquin is responsible to parents, the school district, the general public and the state. Because holistic educational philosophy and parent participation are not widely understood, Charquin must explain and define itself on its own terms (and not allow others to do it). Charquin is vulnerable when it lets its work be defined and explained by an assessment method that was developed for traditional schools. Therefore, Charquin's situation calls for another form of assessment, an appropriate one, which will serve the function of explaining its achievements without violating its philosophy.

Reflections

Building the good school for today's children is above all a community-building task. It's a task which requires that people come together to discuss the technical and ethical problems that they, their students, and children face. If a community is to do this successfully they must revisit Ron Miller's question, *What Are Schools For?* They must struggle with the matter of finding approaches that address the critical issue of preparing children, parents, and teachers to play more powerful roles in reshaping the schools and the society in which they live and work.

The project requires constant evaluation, reflection, and commitment to learning and doing new things. It's a process that depends on holding fast to democratic principles. (While teachers do need to assert their professional leadership, sacrificing democracy to expediency is no way to prepare people to be powerful participants in a democratic society!)

Since the structure of an institution limits and shapes who can do what within it, building the good school requires taking a close look at issues of school structure. A traditionally structured school, where students are separated by grade level and teachers are isolated from one another, inhibits community-building activities. Furthermore, it provides little opportunity for parents to participate fully: to share their stories, provide instruction, make decisions, and learn new things.

Most parents need the support of a school community and the support of other parents and teachers, or they soon burn out and quit coming to school. A more democratic structure not only encourages community-building, but allows individual parents the latitude that they need in order to more fully share their gifts with children—thereby making participation a more challenging and fulfilling enterprise.

Charquin doesn't focus on changing parents. Once parents become powerfully involved they change—and so does the program. Today's schools are badly out of step because they are rigidly structured autocracies bent on fixing people. This posture deters participation. In democratically structured institutions reform is built into the system, and the freedom and responsibility of individuals within that system are respected. The features of Charquin's structure that seem most helpful in encouraging parent participation are:

Multi-age grouping, which makes it possible for a parent to spend several years developing his skills, interests, and teaching style, before moving on to another classroom. Multi-age grouping also makes it possible for parents to observe the developmental continuum in a group of children—thereby gaining confidence in the developmental process.

Team teaching brings the talents of several professionals to bear on program development and creates a more consistent program over time.

Schools within schools is a management system that allows teams of teachers to focus on a manageable number of students and parents and makes direct democracy a viable tool for governing the group.

The Parent Group and its various committees enables parents to participate in the decision-making that effects the conditions of their participation and the quality of their children's education. Parent committees are powerful tools for community-building and parent education.

The case for learning centers is mixed, and their effectiveness depends upon careful management. On the one hand they allow parents to focus their participation in areas where they are most competent and effective. On the other hand, centers can focus the program on individualized choices, rather than co-operative projects. They can also contribute to artificial divisions among disciplines and a disjointed curriculum. Unit planning—while always important—has special urgency when learning centers are a central feature of the program.

The issues of program scale and age span continue to be troubling for Charquin. Generally speaking, the problem of governing the program in a democratic way became more difficult as the program grew from thirty to ninety students and included a wider span of ages. The problem was exacerbated by the large class sizes in Hayward schools—over thirty students per teacher. (A class size of twenty-five would have meant a program size of seventy-five rather than ninety two or three—and correspondingly fewer parents to interact with the teachers.)

Having two parent groups, one for older children and one for younger children, would have relieved the concerns of parents and teachers about the developmental appropriateness of the program for children of different ages. This would be accomplished at the expense of having some parents participating in two groups for at least part of their tenure in the program. It would also have implications for how students are transitioned from the younger to the older group.

Other issues that are not yet settled are those of assessment of student progress and the employment and evaluation of teachers. Teacher hiring and evaluation are particularly troubling problems at this time. Historically Charquin parents have interviewed and had a strong say in the employment of program teachers. In the last several years, the administration has used massive lay-offs of teachers in the district as an excuse to suspend this practice. Furthermore, the district has appointed teachers to fill vacancies at Charquin without considering whether the teacher is commited to a holistic, parent participation philosophy. This is a life threatening matter for the program.

When considering what meaning might be attached to the Charquin story, it seems necessary to say up front several things that this book is not. The Charquin story is not an argument that all schools can or should become little Charquins, or that Charquin should be held up as a standard for other schools. Different schools have different situations and should work things out in different ways.

The Charquin story is not an argument for parent participation as a means of cheap school reform. It isn't about having parents doing the teachers' work. Parent participation demands a higher level of professionalism from teachers. If we are serious about having good schools for our children we must pay for the best teachers, respect them, and support them.

The Charquin story isn't an argument for tearing down all of our schools and starting over. It does suggest that adequate classroom space is important. Thoughtful use of space—including hallway and outdoor spaces—and the cutting of doors between some classrooms will make most old classrooms functional.

This book is not an argument for setting up more alternative schools and magnet schools—or for promoting Public Schools of Choice. While choice is an element in school quality, Public Schools of Choice, as promoted by President Bush and William Bennett, is a way of avoiding the debate surrounding the question of what schools are for. It assumes that anything will work—which seems absurd—and pays little attention to parent participation. Public Schools of Choice holds the potential for further disadvantaging the already disadvantaged, many of whom lack the resources to avail themselves of the choices. Public Schools of Choice, while offering parents an officially sanctioned menu, might actually disempower parents by closing them out when issues of philosophy, program design, and access are debated in the district office.

Involving parents in school reform means involving them in a highly political task. Many people have a stake in the status quo and are afraid of change. As Sharon Rich said (in Manning & Manning, 226), "Whole Language in its best sense is frightening because it implies restructuring of traditional schools and an opening of the curriculum with parent education as a part of the total school package." In addressing the fear of change that teachers and parents bring with them, those approaches that are rooted in democratic process, community-building, and an enlightened sharing of information within the community will be most successful.

The Whole Language Movement has started out by supporting teacher training projects that encourage teachers to try more holistic methods. The hope is that eventually teachers will see the underlying implications of the methods they enjoy, and that they will come together with other teachers and with parents to restructure the schools in which they work.

Enlightened political leadership is needed. Well thought-out federal and state programs could be incentives for reform. On the other hand, inappropriate public policy, such as mandating standardized tests and standardized curriculum, could be a serious deterrent to productive reform. Charter schools will be helpful in changing the culture of schools only to the extent that they are carefully studied, well reported, and not allowed to serve elitist interests.

Any productive public policy will have to take into account the necessity of a different type of teacher training—one that focuses on process and collaboration. Public policy must also recognize that different school communities will have different challenges and different resources with which to work as they endeavor to develop Whole Language schools and encourage parent participation. Most schools will have to hold parent education workshops. In some schools professional parent educators, or ombudsmen, may be needed on staff to assist teachers in committee work and parent education. In poor districts parents may need to ride the school buses and take advantage of school meal programs.

In more advantaged communities a dedicated principal and a couple of experienced teachers may be able to guide and encourage the programs while offering little material support.

The Charquin Story is an argument for making an investment, for becoming personally involved, for restructuring the system to involve parents in all phases of program development, and for doing the best that we can for all children. This story shows that parent empowerment only begins when a choice is made. Real empowerment comes from expressing one's commitment through participation.

At Charquin parents are allowed to try things out, make mistakes, reflect on and discuss what they have learned, and construct their own knowledge of who they are and what they can do. In other words, parent education is guided by the same holistic, participatory, developmental philosophy that guides the children's program. Parents engage in a process. It's not an efficient process. It's an intensely democratic process. It's a process that newcomers have difficulty trusting and being part of — for which they need much support.

Charquin teachers must read the research, debate the issues, try new things, and speak with a professional voice on matters of teaching and learning. The success of Charquin teachers is intricately entwined with the success of the parents. At Charquin parents and teachers become collaborators in the enterprise of educating themselves, their students, and their children for powerful participation in a changing world.

The challenge that schools face today is that of empowering all parents, students, and teachers. The Charquin experience is worthy of note, not because it's a perfect program that has addressed all the issues, but because Charquin demonstrates a process which shows promise of transforming the way that we think about and act within schools. It's a process which underlines the importance of structural issues and for bringing parents into full participation in their children's education.

References

Introduction

Altwerger, Bess. "Whole Language: What's New?" In *Whole Language: Beliefs and Practices, K-8,* Edited by G. Manning, and M. Manning. Washington, D.C.: National Education Association, July, 1989.

Bellah, Robert, R. Madsen, W. M. Sullivan, A. Swidler, and S. M. Tipton. *The Good Society.* New York: Vintage Books, 1991.

Charquin: A Guide to the Operation of Charquin. Hayward, CA: Charquin Alternative Education Program, Hayward Unified School District, 1990.

Clark, Edward T. "The Search For a New Educational Paradigm: The Implications of New Assumptions about Thinking and Learning." *Holistic Education Review* (Spring 1988) 18-30.

Forbes, Jack. *Native Americans of California and Nevada,* rev. ed., Happy Camp, CA: Naturegraph, 1982.

Goodlad, John I. *A Place Called School: Prospects for the Future.* New York: McGraw-Hill, 1984.

Goodman, Ken. *What's Whole About Whole Language?* Portsmouth, NH: Heinemann Educational Books, 1986.

Henderson, Anne. *The Evidence Continues to Grow: Parent Involvement Improves Student Achievement.* Washington, D.C.:National Committee for Citizens in Education (NCCE), 1987.

Manning, Maryann, G. Manning, and C. Kamii. "Early Phonics Instruction: Its Effect on Literacy Development." *Young Children* (November 1988).

McCallum, Richard. *Don't Fence Me In: The Impact of Alternative Management Decisions on Student Achievement in the Charquin Program.* Berkeley: University of California, 1986.

Miller, Ron. *What Are Schools For? Holistic Education in American Culture*. Brandon, VT: Holistic Education Press, 1990.

Newman, Judith M. *Whole Language: Theory in Use*. Portsmouth, N.H.: Heinemann Educational Books, 1985.

Sherr, Mary-Lou Breitborde. "Teaching the Politics of Literacy: Notes from a 'Methods' Course." *Holistic Education Review*. (Spring 1990) 17-20.

Smiley, Frederick M. "Usable Pasts and Unlimited Futures: A Discussion on Selected Tenets of Whole Language." *Holistic Education Review* 3 (Fall 1990): 8-11.

U.S. Department of Labor. The Secretary's Commission on Achieving Necessary Skills. *What Work Requires of Schools*. A Scans Report for America 2000. Washington, D.C.: 1991.

Whitlow, R.F., *Instructional Materials and Teacher Change: Confessions of a Liberated Teacher*. (unpublished) 1990.

"Good Morning"

Postman, Neil, and Charles Weingartner. *The School Book: For People Who Want to Know What All the Hollering is About*. New York: Delacorte Press, 1973.

"The Basics"

Gentry, Richard J. *Spel is a Four Letter Word*. Portsmouth, N.H.: Heinemann Educational Books, 1987.

Graves, Donald H. *Writing: Teachers and Children at Work*. Exeter, N.H.: Heinemann Educational Books, 1983.

Whitlow, R.F. *Instructional Materials and Teacher Change: Confessions of a Liberated Teacher,* (unpublished) 1990.

The Parent Group

Curran, Dolores. *Traits of a Healthy Family,* Minneapolis: Winston Press, 1983.

Tradition and Development

Bakalis, Michael. "It Works This Way for Some: Case Studies of Fifteen Schools." In *Alternative Education: A Source Book for Parents, Teachers, Students, and Administrators,* edited by Mario Fantini. Garden City, NY: Anchor Books, 1976.

Deal, Terrence E. "An Organizational Explanation of the Failure of Alternative Schools," *Research and Development Memorandum, No. 133,* Stanford Center for Research and Development in Teaching (February 1975).

Forbes, Jack. *Native Americans of California and Nevada,* rev. ed., Happy Camp, CA: Naturegraph, 1982.

Keen, Sam, and Anne Valley-Fox. *Your Mythic Journey: Finding Meaning in Your Life Through Writing and Storytelling.* Los Angeles: Jeremy P. Tarcher, 1989.

Assessment

Goodman, Ken S., Lois Bridges Bird, and Yetta M. Goodman. *The Whole Language Catalog.* Santa Rosa, CA: American School Publishers, 1991.

Goodman, Ken S., Yetta M. Goodman, and Wendy J. Hood. *The Whole Language Evaluation Book.* Portsmouth, NH: Heinemann, 1988.

Reflections

Rich, Sharon. "Restoring Power to Teachers: The Impact of 'Whole Language.'" In *Whole Language: Beliefs and Practices, K-8,* edited by G. Manning and M. Manning. Washington, D.C.: National Education Association. July, 1989.

Index

Order Form

Please send me____ copies of Building the Good
School:*Participating Parents at Charquin* at
$14.95 per copy.

Total Amount ordered $ _____

*Alameda County residents
please add 8.25% sales tax* _____

*Other California residents
add 7.25% sales tax* _____

Subtotal _____

*Add Postage and handling
$2.00 for first copy, $.75
for each additional copy* _____

Send Orders to: TOTAL _____

**Ohlone Press
Post Office Box 779
Hayward, California 94543-0779
Telephone:(510)537-3439**   **Please Print**

Date_____

_____
First Name   Middle Initial   Last Name

_____
Organization   Department

_____
Street Mailing Address

_____
City   State   Zip

Thank you for your order!